SILICON
AND THE
STATE

SILICON
AND THE
STATE

French Innovation Policy
in the Internet Age

GUNNAR TRUMBULL

BROOKINGS INSTITUTION PRESS
Washington, D.C.

Library of Congress Cataloging-in-Publication data
Trumbull, Gunnar.
  Silicon and the State : French innovation policy in the Internet age / Gunnar
Trumbull.
      p. cm.
  Includes bibliographical references (p.   ) and index.
  ISBN 0-8157-8596-8 (cloth : alk. paper)
  ISBN 0-8157-8597-6 (pbk. : alk. paper)
  1. Information technology--Government policy–France. 2. Technological
innovations–Government policy–France. 3. Industrial policy–France.
4. Internet–Government policy–France. I. Title.
  HC280.I55T78 2004
  338'.064'0944–dc22   2004000194

9 8 7 6 5 4 3 2 1

Typeset in Sabon

Composition by Stephen D. McDougal
Mechanicsville, Maryland

Printed by R. R. Donnelley
Harrisonburg, Virginia

To Betty Lee Trumbull

Contents

Foreword

This book brings together two subjects that have been prominently on the agenda of the Brookings Institution in recent years: globalization and France. During the 1990s, the economic life of the planet became more integrated than ever before as trade, capital, people, and information increasingly flowed across state borders—a trend that Brookings scholars have studied in a variety of projects and publications, many of them interdisciplinary. And in 1999, we established the Brookings Center on the United States and France, which in April 2004 became a program within our new Center on the United States and Europe, directed by Senior Fellow Philip Gordon. Gunnar Trumbull's *Silicon and the State*, written while Trumbull was a visiting fellow at Brookings, examines an important dimension of how France is adapting to globalization, adding to other recent Brookings volumes such as Gordon's book with Sophie Meunier, *The French Challenge* (2001); and Hubert Védrine's *France in an Age of Globalization* (2000).

Globalization put pressure on nearly every country in the world to adapt their economic and cultural institutions to the competitive needs of the world economy. The United States, with its booming economy and a seemingly inexhaustible capacity for innovation, served as the model. The message from consultants and gurus the world over was, in short, emulate the United States or suffer economic decline. Silicon Alleys, Silicon Fens, and even Silicon Bogs sprouted up throughout the world as conscious efforts to import an American model that harnessed venture capital, light state regulation, and entrepreneurial dynamism to create cutting edge innovation and ultimately technology-led economic growth.

Nowhere was this conventional wisdom better understood or more resented than in France. That country remains the proud home of a state-led model of capitalism that is the antithesis of America's individualistic model of development. The pressures of globalization in France (where it is often seen as synonymous with "Americanization") created a powerful anti-globalization movement, generated grand pronouncements of cultural protection from politicians, and even spurred violence against symbols of American industry such as McDonald's. Thomas Friedman, the *New York Times* columnist, summarized the American view on these events in his 2000 best-seller, *The Lexus and the Olive Tree*. He ranked countries' prospects according to their ability to adapt American-inspired globalization and concluded "Buy Taiwan, Hold Italy, Sell France."

In retrospect, however, "selling France" would have been a mistake. In this examination of French technology policy, Gunnar Trumbull demonstrates how French officials, against the backdrop of public anti-globalization rhetoric, consciously set out to reconcile the need for a new dynamism in the French economy with France's historical commitment to state-led economic policy and thus create an alternative to the American model of innovation that could compete and even prosper in the modern world economy. Beginning in 1997, French government officials undertook an extraordinary state-led project to remake France into a country of entrepreneurs. They created powerful tax incentives for investment in risky ventures, streamlined state regulation of small business, wrote new company laws to favor venture capital, and encouraged high-tech start-ups. In a country that had previously developed new technologies through state-owned firms, the transformation was dramatic and controversial, generating substantial resistance from both consumers and industry.

It is still too early to assess the economic consequences of this experiment. But Trumbull's analysis already offers some important lessons to countries attempting to both adapt to globalization and preserve their most cherished institutions. Most important, and most paradoxically, he argues, promoting individual economic entrepreneurship in a country with strong social commitments requires policy entrepreneurship from the state. For France, the incentives necessary to encourage risky ventures confronted basic cultural values such as a deep commitment to social and economic equity. Opponents of the reforms worried that they would undermine social norms of risk sharing, increase income inequalities, and even threaten France's immensely popular public pension plan. New policies therefore had to be creatively crafted in order to address such concerns without stifling entrepreneurial activity. Indeed, one of the ironies of the French experience is that making entrepreneurship politically acceptable required in some cases more rather than less government intervention. For France, as for every other nation on Earth, embracing globalization was a necessity, but as in all things, French policymakers wanted to do it their way— and that doesn't mean blindly following the American model. Or, as they would say, *Vive la difference.*

STROBE TALBOTT
President

Washington, D.C.
February 2004

Acknowledgments

I would like to thank a number of people who have read and commented on various parts and stages of the manuscript, including Suzanne Berger, Steve Casper, Pepper Culpepper, Keith Darden, Vincent Dessain, Marie-Laure Djelic, Orfeo Fioretos, Ethan Kapstein, Eugene Gholz, Philip Gordon, Isabela Mares, Jeremy Shapiro, James Steinberg, Seema Tikare, and Nicholas Ziegler.

For generously taking time to share their insights on recent changes in the French political economy, I am especially grateful to Godefroy Beauvallet, Stéphane Boujnah, Michel Gilbaud, Guy Carrèrre, Fabrice Cavarretta, Philippe Collombel, Antoine Décitre, Benoît Habert, Laurent Kott, Nicolas Landrin, Michel Meyer, Olivier Protard, Jean-Noël Tronc, François Véron, and Nicolas Véron, as well as several others who requested that they not be identified.

I would like to give special thanks to the Brookings Institution, to its Center on the United States and France, and especially to the Center's director, Philip Gordon, for his continuing support and encouragement on this project. I would also like to thank the Harvard Business School and its European Research Center for their support and assistance. Of course, the views expressed here are solely mine and should not be ascribed to the persons above or to the trustees, officers, or other staff members of Brookings.

Finally, for their endless support and friendship, I thank my wife, Seema Tikare, my parents, Betty and James Trumbull, and my brothers, Nat and Sam Trumbull.

CHAPTER ONE

Technology
and the State

Frrance in the late 1990s undertook a revolution in innovation policy. Afraid of falling behind the liberal market systems of the United States and the United Kingdom, the cohabitation government of Prime Minister Lionel Jospin and President Jacques Chirac put in place a vast array of new policies—from tax incentives for investing in risky high-tech start-ups to new standards for electronic signatures—designed to promote new information and communications technologies in France. In their analysis, France in the 1990s had succeeded in the basic sciences, but failed to translate laboratory findings into commercially viable new technologies. Roger-Gérard Schwartzenberg, French minister of research, described France's apparent economic lag as emerging "not from a lack of gray matter, but from an incomplete exploitation and valuation of resources."[1]

The French leadership was especially concerned about a brain drain, as France's technically trained elite increasingly moved to join vibrant small-firm sectors that already existed in Britain and the United States.[2] With its new policies the government sought to encourage the commercialization of new technologies, and they looked to the United States to understand how this might be done. What they found was that in the cutting-edge sectors that constituted the "new economy"—biotechnology, information and communications technology, e-commerce—the successful exploitation of basic science findings appeared to depend on a context of dynamic, new, innovative firms funded through private venture capital. Preoccupied by a growing technology lag, and driven by the fear of losing highly trained technicians to foreign firms, France was determined to create a domestic analog to Silicon Valley.

The new set of technology policies France put in place turned French innovation policy on its head. Traditional government and bank-financed research and development were progressively replaced by private venture capital. France's technical elite, long accustomed to a secure career track in France's prestigious laboratories and industrial conglomerates, were encouraged to move into risky new companies. New technologies that had once been developed in France's prestigious industrial conglomerates were now being commercialized by small technology start-ups. Much of this effort was focused on start-ups working in the new information and communications sectors.

But France's homegrown analog to Silicon Valley, if it did succeed, was likely to look different from its American counterpart in at least two ways. First, France's new technology start-ups did not emerge spontaneously. Drawing on the French interventionist regulatory tradition, the government played a guiding role in establishing the basis for high-tech innovation in the private sector. Efforts included public contests and educational programs to promote entrepreneurship, industry incubators sponsored by public research labs, even an entirely new legal form for companies tailored to the needs of high-tech start-ups. The goal was to create a new institutional framework in which individual entrepreneurship could prosper. But encouraging small-firm dynamism appeared, at least at the outset, to imply more rather than less state activism.

Second, French policymakers faced strong political pressure to make the new innovation strategy compatible with French political values of equality and social solidarity. Government efforts to promote entrepreneurship were therefore carefully designed to limit their impact on French society. Stock options in France were tightly regulated to balance incentives for innovation against excessive executive compensation. The administrative burden on French companies was reduced, but not through simple deregulation. Instead, the French *service publique* began adopting Internet-based capabilities to streamline business interaction with the government. And new private investment instruments were carefully designed so that they would not threaten France's popular public welfare system. Even as the French government encouraged private innovation via start-ups working in new technology sectors, it retained a strong guiding role for itself in the economy.

This book investigates France's experience in adapting to the requirements of innovation in the new information and communications technology (ICT) sectors. It focuses on the six-year period from 1996 to 2002. Although short in duration, this period included dramatic efforts at regulatory reform; a boom in technology start-ups, venture capital, and initial public offerings (IPOs); the spread of the Internet, then a collapse in the Internet market, accompanied by a broader economic decline. This short stretch of time, in other words, was a crucible for French leaders and businesspeople, a period in which the new challenges of the ICT revolution were confronted, when new policies and practices were tested and stressed.

Of course, the challenges that the new information and communications technologies posed were not unique to France. All countries, in one way or another, faced the same issues. But by focusing on the experience of a single country, we can gain a deeper sense of the political and economic challenges of adjustment, and of the interests that lay behind the policies. It may be many years before we are able accurately to assess the economic consequences of the experiment that France undertook during this six-year period. But we can already capture the political and social texture of the struggle. To understand the challenge that new technologies pose to sovereignty, we need to look where silicon and the state collided.

Technology and the State

Observers have suggested that today's new information and communications technologies constitute an industrial revolution. On a par with the mechanization of the eighteenth century or the vertical integration pioneered in the nineteenth century, this third industrial revolution threatens to change the very economic and social order of society.[3] Like these earlier revolutions, the new ICT may fundamentally reshape industry and the workplace.[4] Researchers at the Berkeley Roundtable on the International Economy describe the new ICT as "producing one of those very rare eras in which advanced technology and changing organizations do not revolutionize just one leading economic sector but transform the entire economy and ultimately the rest of society as well."[5] But in one important respect this latest revolution appeared to be different from its predecessors. Despite the political challenges that earlier industrial revolutions posed, they left the state stronger and the nation more consolidated. The third industrial revolution, by contrast, appeared to threaten core functions of the state.

The French state historically played a central role in developing and commercializing new technologies. These new technologies in turn promoted, rather than subverted, the purposes of the state. France's earliest communications technology, the visual telegraph invented by the Chappe brothers, employed a chain of tall towers sporting mechanical semaphore arms. The system was used to transmit messages from Paris to the limits of French territory. Soon new steel train lines extended along the paths of the semaphore, built in a radial pattern extending from Paris, accompanied by the new electrical telegraph. Such projects have been deeply tied to the creation of a distinctive French identity. These early technologies drew the country together as a commercial unit, while also meeting basic military needs to transport troops and materiel to the borders. "There could be no unity," concludes Eugen Weber in *Peasants into Frenchmen*, "before there was national circulation."[6] They helped to create what Benedict Anderson has called an "imagined community," an image of France as a nation of which all were a part.[7]

Not only did new technologies reinforce the French state; the state was also the primary sponsor and user of new technologies. Especially in the post–World War II period, emerging technologies were systematically pursued and applied to reinforce national sovereignty. The new technologies increased the power and autonomy of the French state in two ways. As complex and technologically challenging projects, they required a deep government role in the promotion of new research. This has been especially true in the post–World War II era. The elite National Center for Scientific Research (Centre national de la recherche scientifique, CNRS), founded in 1939 on the eve of World War II, created a network of re-search labs intended explicitly to support basic research in the national interest. Through CNRS the postwar French state was able to direct the development of new technologies.

Moreover, the technologies often had explicitly national goals. Mili-tary research allowed France to manufacture advanced weapons. Space launch technology gave France worldwide surveillance capacity. France also pursued an aggressive nuclear power program in order to reduce its energy dependency on the Middle East. When France withdrew from NATO in 1966, for example, the United States refused to sell advanced computers to assist with France's nuclear research. In response, Charles de Gaulle created a new national laboratory in advanced computing, the Institut national de la recherche en informatique et en automatique (INRIA), located in the abandoned NATO headquarters in Rocquencourt.[8] Research at INRIA in turn laid the groundwork for France's homegrown computer manufacturer, Bull. Thus both in their development and in their use, the new technologies of the second half of the twentieth century served to concentrate and reinforce the French state's control over key technolo-gies. In doing so they helped to forge a modern French identity grounded in national autonomy, cohesiveness, and a respect for state initiative.

And what was good for the state appeared to be good for industry. Since the 1950s, French industrial innovation projects have been ambi-tious and largely successful.[9] That success had its roots in large state-run companies, so-called national champions, which received high levels of government financial and research support. The Ariane space launch ve-hicles, Airbus and the *Concorde*, France's nuclear program, Minitel, Renault automobiles—nearly all of France's industrial achievements of the postwar period had their origins in collaborative projects between France's large firms and the state. The relationship between large and small firms was correspondingly troubled.[10] If anything, French planners typically tried to eliminate small companies, in the understanding that they lacked the market power and economies of scale necessary for pro-moting economic efficiency.[11]

But the features of the French political economy that so closely aligned the interests of the technology sector and the state also posed challenges for promoting innovation in the new information and communications sectors. France's tradition of state-initiated innovation tended to concentrate France's technical "knowledge-bearing" elite within the state-run sectors. Those with the greatest capacity for technological innovation were still mainly working for the government.[12] On top of this, the postwar tradition of state-led industrial planning and the apparent success of earlier government-funded innovation projects had led French citizens to associate innovation with government initiative.[13] But this legacy confronted the French state with a conundrum. On the one hand, government-led initiatives were poorly suited to the rapid pace of technological and market development in the new information and communications technologies. France's Plan Calcul to promote the electronics sector in the 1960s and 1970s had already shown that state-sponsored innovation did not necessarily compete well in the global marketplace for information technologies.[14] On the other hand, if new private initiatives failed, it was likely that these failures would nonetheless be blamed on the government. Moreover, the dominant role of the central government in postwar France had weakened local authorities that might otherwise have taken the lead in promoting decentralized private-sector innovation projects.[15] France's postwar economic trajectory had concentrated expertise, political responsibility, and institutional capacity at the state level. This posed real problems for cultivating technology-intensive innovation in small firms.

The Challenge of New Information Technologies

Moving to a decentralized model of innovation in order to make France competitive in the new information technologies required potentially risky changes in policy. Would private investors make appropriate decisions about the allocation of venture capital? Would entrepreneurs acting separately pursue projects that generated a successful technological trajectory for France? Could the government legitimately step back from technology decisions that were arguably critical for France's economic future?

French politicians expressed real concerns about whether their country could adopt the institutions necessary to promote high-tech start-ups without at the same time importing the entire package of American-style capitalism. "How can we catch up with the United States," asked Christian Sautter, Jospin's former economics minister, "without losing our souls, that is, without sacrificing the solidarity that lies at the heart of the European model?"[16] The centerpiece of the ICT revolution, the Internet, was grounded in a collection of new technologies and services—microelectronics, software, telecommunications; Internet service providers, e-tailers, and web designers—that appeared to prosper only in a liberal economy. Yet France had, until recently, possessed few of the necessary liberal economic institutions.

Venture capital funds, a central source of start-up capital, were invented in the United States in 1954. They did not appear in significant numbers in France until forty years later. Stock-option plans had become a core component of compensation for technology entrepreneurs in the United States, luring highly skilled scientists, engineers, and businesspeople into risky ventures with the promise of future fortune. But French tax law had recently been rewritten to make stock options prohibitively expensive. Finally, a successful high-tech start-up sector implied the rapid formation and dissolution of companies. The U.S. common law legal system and its tradition of laissez-faire regulation imposed low costs on company creation and failure. France's civil code legal system and strong regulatory tradition, in contrast, placed brakes on company creation and failure.

The risks implicit in a small-firm technology sector also challenged basic tenets of France's social contract: risk-sharing, job security, and wage equality. Entrepreneurs and investors in the new economy would face high levels of financial risk. On the one hand, this high level of risk would drive a rapid cycle of company formation and failure that challenged France's traditional emphasis on job security and the socialization of risk. On the other hand, the high-powered incentives necessary to draw scientists and investors into risky ventures would create a new class of affluent French, a prospect that implied widening inequalities. France's efforts to promote a French Silicon Valley therefore generated a heated political debate focused on its compatibility with France's implicit—and occasionally very explicit—social contract.

Policymakers and public intellectuals feared that the liberal policies required for success in the new economy might be the thin edge of an unstoppable deregulatory wedge. Alain Minc argued in his best-selling *www.capitalisme.fr* that a market economy would necessarily lead to a market society: "The principles of the market . . . competition [and] the continuous evaluation of performance, penetrate into broader and broader spheres of society. It becomes, over the course of time, a market society."[17] Critics like Minc argued that the logic of market liberalism could not be embraced halfway, that it would eventually come to dominate all of French life. Anglo-American commercial culture was held up as a cautionary example of what French society could become if it embraced the ideology of the "new economy" and its technologies: a society in which markets alone dictated the terms of work, of leisure, and of national culture.

Sources of French Policy Activism

The new emphasis on promoting high-tech start-ups in France had its roots in three sets of domestic concerns: France's poor performance in new economy sectors, high unemployment, and a political desire by the incoming administration to appear engaged in the economy. In the first instance, French leadership was responding to concerns over an apparent innovation lag in France. The incoming Jospin government saw clear signs that French industrial innovation had declined in the 1990s. The French share of patents issued in the United States had fallen from 3.03 percent of all patents in the period 1991–94 to 2.72 percent in the period 1995–98. France also had relatively fewer researchers than other countries, accounting for just 5.9 percent of the work force, compared with 7.4 percent in the United States and 8.3 percent in Japan.[18] The government was particularly concerned about innovation in the high-technology sectors, especially ICT and biotechnology. France contributed only 2.5 percent of the total cost of research to the human genome project, for example, whereas 33 percent came from Britain and 55 percent from the United States.[19] And it trailed its major European rivals in levels of computer and Internet use both in business and in the general population. Because ICT and biotechnology sectors both appeared to rely on small, dynamic companies to create and commercialize new products, the French government saw small-firm innovation as a core component of its national innovation strategy.

Perhaps more important than the innovation lag, however, was the prospect of new job creation that the small-firm sector offered. The Jospin government came to power with a mandate to lower France's stubbornly high rate of unemployment. Newly created firms in the technology sectors were seen as a particularly important source of new jobs. Indeed one in five private sector employees in France worked in a company that was less than five years old.[20] A study conducted in 1995 showed that technology companies formed by researchers created three times as many new jobs as did other kinds of new companies.[21] Another study on the economic impact of innovation found that the new technology sectors had contributed 35 percent of the growth of the U.S. economy between 1995 and 1998, while the new economy sectors in France accounted for only 20 percent of overall economic growth.[22] The promotion of a new high-technology sector dominated by successful small firms offered not only the prospect of rapid new job creation, but also a set of new jobs in high-wage, high-skill areas of the economy.

Interest in promoting innovation and job creation through technology start-ups was especially strong because it came in the wake of a decade-long decline in company creation in France (see figure 1-1). New firm creation had fallen almost continuously over the previous decade, from 320,000 new firms created in 1989 to 255,000 new firms created in 1999. Germany, in comparison, saw the creation of 390,000 new companies in 1999. Indeed France had the lowest rate of new company formation, per capita, in Europe.[23] The outlook for new firms in France was not entirely negative. After 1996, a relative drop in company failures offset the decline in company creations, so the total number of firms in France grew after 1996. A comparison with Britain showed that new French firms at the time were far more likely to succeed than were their British counterparts. In France, 57 percent of new firms lasted at least five years; only 37 percent did so in Britain.[24] The problem was that the Silicon Valley model relied both on rapid new firm creation *and* on the possibility of rapid firm failure, and France's economy seemed to enjoy neither of these.

Beyond these economic reasons for pursuing a small-firm technology strategy, there was also a political logic. The Jospin administration came into office on the premise that policy activism could address France's economic woes. In 1995, François Mitterrand had announced, "We have tried everything. Nothing works against unemployment." Jospin's campaign strategy had been to repudiate Mitterrand's fatalism. Once in office, his administration was dedicated to the idea that the government *could* do something.[25] This was the political logic behind the new government's

Figure 1-1.   *Company Creation and Failure in France, 1989–98*

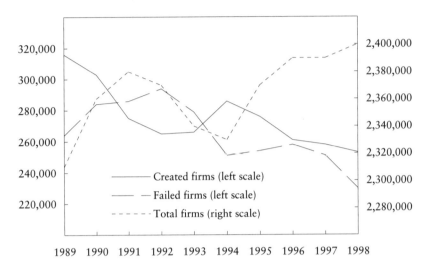

Source: Christian Cordellier, "Créations et cessations d'entreprises: sous la stabilité, le renouvellement," *INSEE Première*, no. 740 (October 2000), p. 1.

emphasis on small-firm innovation.[26] A focus on new technologies would highlight differences not only with the Mitterrand legacy but also with the previous administration of Alain Juppé, which was perceived not to have emphasized technology. When the Jospin group took over in 1997, almost no one in the French ministries used e-mail, and the Internet was essentially unknown. La Villette, France's advanced technology showplace northeast of Paris, had explicitly banned the Internet from its displays. Thus for the Socialists coming into power, a new technology emphasis allowed them to seem both activist and modern. And, critically, the new technology policies promised to be inexpensive. In an explicit understanding between Prime Minister Lionel Jospin and Economics Minister Dominique Strauss-Kahn, Jospin agreed to put his political weight behind the new information and communications technologies, but to give them minimal financial support.[27]

Policy Entrepreneurship

Rather than pursuing a path of deregulation modeled on the U.S. experience, the Socialist government that came into power in 1997 pursued an activist policy to promote the information and communications technologies. The Jospin team worked methodically to redraw economic incentives and barriers so as to promote entrepreneurship, but in a way that would be compatible with the social and economic obligations of the French state. These reforms, which in most instances amounted to reregulation rather than deregulation of the economy, allowed France to find its own way in the globalized economy.[28] The U.S. experience, as one French venture capitalist expressed it, was more of a benchmark than a model.[29]

In reforming the regulatory framework for entrepreneurship, the French government paid close attention to the interest and advice of economic actors. Speaking of the need for new rules in a globalized economy, Dominique Strauss-Kahn, finance minister under Jospin, said: "These new rules will not only be statist: they will also involve the social partners."[30] One forum for this involvement was the new Council of Economic Analysis (Conseil d'analyse économique, CAE). Created July 24, 1997, the CAE included thirty-two professional economists and was headed by the prime minister. Unlike the U.S. Council of Economic Advisers, the CAE was nonpartisan. Its representatives came from different parties and positions, some even from outside France. In this sense it looked more like its German neighbor, the council of "five wise men," who were politically neutral and diverse in perspective. Because the CAE deliberated in private, it avoided much of the political conflict that the five wise men often generated. Prime Minister Jospin called the new group a *boîte à idées*, or think tank, to the government.[31] It undertook studies of issues such as unemployment, government contracting, and the "new economy." Jospin's successor, Jean-Pierre Raffarin, was less attentive to the CAE, and reportedly considered merging it with France's traditional economic planning agency, the Commissariat général du plan. Ultimately it was left in place, but with less influence.[32]

The French Senate sought its own source of input through a new program of Senatorial Meetings with Industry (Rencontres sénatoriales de l'entreprise). Its goal was "to better understand the evolution of the economy, to listen to corporate actors, and to see the concrete impact of legislation."[33] From October to December 2000, for example, forty-one senators visited companies for one to three days. The companies covered the spectrum from start-ups to multinationals, and nine of these were in the Internet economy.[34] Legislation written in the Sénat, including corporate governance reform and the reregulation of stock options, was informed by these visits.[35]

New organizations also emerged to represent the positions of the growing entrepreneurial class. The lobbying group Croissance Plus, created in 1997 by Pierre Harin, pushed for government support for activities in the new technology sectors. Croissance Plus included 150 individual members from new technology firms.[36] Cofounder Benoît Habert, for example, was president of the venture capital fund of Dassault Développement. Among other activities, the group invited political figures to discuss their views on the new economy. Interestingly, the sources of technology lobbying were not only domestic. The group Objectif 2010, organized by Philippe Pouletty, an immunologist and French entrepreneur who had moved his company SangStat to Silicon Valley, was influential with the Jospin government in the late 1990s. He lobbied against France's wealth tax and helped to design the new company statute to benefit entrepreneurial start-ups. The name of the organization was a reference to its goal: to make France hospitable to entrepreneurs by the year 2010.[37] Another influential group, France Libre d'Entreprendre, was based in Kent, England. Run by Olivier Cadic, an outspoken expatriate critic of the French regulatory and fiscal environment, the group spurred debate in France by helping French companies that wanted to leave France to set up in England.[38] Both of these groups, representing French entrepreneurs in the Anglo-Saxon world, had a powerful voice in shaping the reforms that France put in place.

Perhaps most critical was the way in which Economics Minister Dominique Strauss-Kahn reached out to the business community. A technophile by nature, Strauss-Kahn traveled repeatedly to Silicon Valley. He met with the leaders of American high technology when they came to France, including Steve Jobs (Apple), Bill Gates (Microsoft), John Chambers (Cisco), Michael Dell (Dell), Michael Lynton (AOL), and Eckhard Pfeiffer (Compaq). His special adviser on the new information and communications technologies, Stéphane Boujnah, had been a mergers and acquisitions lawyer at the law firm Freshfields. Boujnah and Strauss-Kahn were able between them to create a strong link between business and government.[39] Indeed without Strauss-Kahn it seems likely that much of the French agenda to promote technology start-ups during this period would not have been launched.

One direction from which France drew little inspiration was the European Union (EU). Although (or perhaps because) the new government technology policies coincided with the push for monetary integration within the EU, France for the most part did not turn to Brussels for solutions to its lag in the new information and communications technologies. There were some exceptions. The European Investment Bank did allocate some resources to new venture capital funds in France. And an effort to benchmark growth of the Internet across Europe was launched following the EU's Lisbon Summit in March 2000. More frequently, though, the EU stood in the way of French efforts. The European Commission, for example, repeatedly criticized tax incentives for investing in French technology firms on the grounds that they were anticompetitive. And EU efforts to create a common framework for Internet commerce largely failed to displace distinctive domestic regulations. Indeed when Jean-Noël Tronc, adviser to Lionel Jospin on the information society, outlined France's strategy for promoting and managing the new information technologies, the European Union was almost entirely absent from his proposed set of policy solutions.[40]

Organization of the Book

Chapters 2 and 3 of this book consider the new institutional context that was created to support highly risky new economy ventures. They argue that the Jospin administration worked to create the functional equivalent of American labor market and financial institutions, but without taking on the entire U.S. economic model. In no case, for example, did France simply pursue a strategy of deregulation. Instead, each policy was negotiated to be politically acceptable to a combination of industry and social interest groups. Complex and often arcane, the regulatory solutions showed signs of having been drafted by committee. Yet they succeeded in creating an institutional context that promoted risky high-technology start-ups without undermining the institutional foundations of French capitalism.

Chapter 2, "The State and the Entrepreneur," focuses on regulations designed to promote small-firm dynamism, including stock options, company law, and the regulatory context of small business. In each area of policy, France put in place complex and novel policy solutions. The treatment of stock options designed to compensate technical entrepreneurs was separated from the treatment of stock options designed to align management incentives with shareholder interests. A new company law format was designed specifically to grant single-owner start-ups greater managerial flexibility. And regulatory reforms designed to ease the administrative burden for small firms focused less on simplifying the regulation and more on streamlining the ways in which companies interact with the government, including via the Internet. These policies struck a careful political balance between the goal of stimulating entrepreneurship and the countervailing goal of maintaining social solidarity.

Chapter 3, "Private Equity in the Shadow of the State," examines the ways in which France promoted private investment in risky technology start-ups. The kind of private venture capital funding that was so successful in promoting high-tech innovation in the United States posed challenges to traditional forms of corporate governance and social security in France. In the United States, venture capital (VC) functioned in close conjunction with active stock markets, since it is through initial public offerings—or acquisition by a large company, typically paid for in company stock—that venture capitalists were able to profit from their risky investments. This Silicon Valley model created two areas of political friction for France. First, the growth of stock markets and equity-financed innovation challenged the traditional bank- and government-financed innovation that characterized much of France's postwar growth. Second, new investment instruments that were created to encourage institutional investment in venture capital funds and in France's new high-tech stock market, the Nouveau Marché, also threatened to become private competitors to France's public pay-as-you-go pension system. Opponents feared that any move toward private pension funds risked undermining the public welfare state while also generating greater income inequality.

Chapters 4 and 5 focus on France's experience with the Internet. France's slow adoption of the new data network technology has commonly been understood as a case study in how government intervention and overregulation can slow the commercialization of new technologies. Chapter 4, "Minitel and the Internet," argues that this view is wrong, and that a combination of market forces and a *lack* of concerted government intervention lay at the core of France's slow Internet growth. France was the only country in the world for which the Internet competed directly with an existing national digital network, the Minitel system. Although Minitel did not offer the services of the Internet, it raised the performance threshold for consumers considering connecting to the Internet. In addition, France's state-owned telephone company, France Télécom, was using its dominant position in the telecommunications business to limit access to the Internet. Indeed it did so despite strong political pressure to lower Internet access rates to a level comparable to those in other European countries.

Chapter 5, "An Internet with Borders," considers the impact of French government regulation of the Internet itself. Despite a small number of highly publicized cases that have highlighted obstructive policies—including the French lawsuit against Yahoo! for selling Nazi memorabilia on its auction site—this chapter argues that France has shown considerable restraint in regulating the Internet. Regulations that *have* been put in place have typically had the goal of securing commercial transactions, thereby encouraging rather than discouraging Internet use. The greatest challenges have emerged in the context of existing French regulations that predate the Internet, concerning anti-Semitism and use of the French language. And even in these instances France has worked to accommodate these concerns with the reality of a global Internet.

Taken together, these chapters reveal that France responded to the significant policy challenges of the new technologies with a state activism that induced, rather than impeded, progress. Instead of stepping back from the economic sphere, the French state redeployed its administrative capacities in new areas. Rather than limiting its influence, the French state continued to play a central role in shaping France's economy.

The solutions that French policymakers chose were not always elegant, and it is too early to know whether they have worked. France's economic slowdown in 2002 hurt the popularity of Jospin's economic reforms. But there are reasons to view the reforms with optimism. First, the more liberal U.S. economy has overseen an extraordinary market-led misallocation of technology resources during this period, and it is against this baseline that the French experience should be evaluated. Second, the French approach offered a response that was at least politically viable. A more liberal set of policy proposals might have faced insurmountable domestic obstacles, leading to retrenchment and inaction rather than reform. Third, the French solution, whatever its flaws, appears to have offered a workable accommodation of French political and social values to the requirements of competitiveness in the new technology sectors. Through careful institutional design, France created the institutional context for a burgeoning start-up sector without destroying those institutions that had long underpinned the French economy. Time will tell whether these accommodations were simply the first stage in a gradual shift toward broader economic liberalization. But the French experience should offer hope for countries that need to make technological dynamism compatible with existing social commitments of the state.

CHAPTER TWO

The State and
the Entrepreneur

French policymakers in the late 1990s worked to create an *entrepreneuriat*, a new class of risk-taking, educated business leaders who would promote new company creation in high-technology sectors. They were trying to induce a transformation from what Jospin's first economics minister, Dominique Strauss-Kahn, described as a culture of rents to a culture of risk. Of course, the idea of promoting entrepreneurship through government activism sounds peculiarly French. But Strauss-Kahn's idea was to create an institutional framework in which entrepreneurs could succeed.[1] To traditionalists on the left and right, these changes were portrayed as "necessary adjustments of traditional state involvement in economic affairs."[2] To economic liberals and potential entrepreneurs, the policies they put in place were seen as revolutionary. Speaking in November 1999 at the "Estates General of Young European Entrepreneurs," organized by the Paris Chamber of Commerce and Industry, President Jacques Chirac described France's new entrepreneurial spirit as "a type of cultural revolution in the strongest sense of the term."[3]

For Americans, the French have been a source of entrepreneurial inspiration. General Georges Doriot founded America's first venture capital fund, American Research and Development (ARD) Corporation, in 1946, and ARD funded Digital Equipment. Fifty years later, Paris-born Pierre Omidyar founded the global online auction site eBay. The vocabulary of

American economic liberalism draws freely on the French language. *Revenue, surplus, laissez-faire,* and, of course, *entrepreneur* all have French roots. Yet France's own political culture has not traditionally embraced the entrepreneur. In 1976, when Prime Minister Raymond Barre faced growing unemployment in the wake of the first oil shock, he called on the French people to create their own jobs: "Let [the unemployed] start their own businesses."[4] French citizens at the time saw this advice as an insult. Echoing Guizot's famous 1840 economic advice, "Enrichissez-vous" (Enrich yourself), Barre seemed to be suggesting the heretical: that employment was not a matter of government responsibility.

Twenty years later, French attitudes toward entrepreneurship appeared to be changing. A survey conducted in January 2000 found that 13 million French citizens over 18 years of age hoped to create their own company over the course of their careers, up from only 3 million who felt similarly inclined in 1992.[5] Interest was particularly strong among the youth. The January 2000 survey found that, of respondents age 18 to 24, 61 percent hoped to create their own company.[6] Even the term *entrepreneur*—coined by the nineteenth-century French economist Jean-Baptiste Say—was coming into a new vogue in France. Commonly used to deprecate a person seen as mischievous or obstreperous, the word increasingly came to connote an exciting life-style that incorporated cell phones and erratic hours. Even France's political elite espoused the cultural shift. President Chirac was seen meeting with sneaker-shod Internet start-up founders and displaying his skills with the computer pointer (a public relations stunt that earned him the moniker Jacques "the mouse" Chirac).[7] But this bold new cultural vision also confronted deeply embedded social and economic interests.

High-Powered Compensation

France in the late 1990s confronted concerns about a brain drain. The number of French citizens living abroad had grown, from 1.64 million in 1995 to 1.78 million in 1998. Over half of these lived in other countries of Western Europe; 20 percent had moved to the United States. This trend was of particular concern to France's leaders because the emigrants were overwhelmingly young and highly educated. A study of the problem commissioned by France's Senate found that nearly one-third (31 percent) of these expatriates belonged to "management and intellectual professions."[8] More frightening for the government, a survey of small-business owners conducted by Ifop in 1999 found that 48 percent were "ready to consider moving all or part of their company abroad."[9] Like the Soviet Union in 1990, France in the mid-1990s had become an attractive place for foreign firms to harvest highly skilled engineers and scientists. The flight of France's technically skilled youth was partly an insult to national pride, partly a loss of tax revenues.

Yet at the same time, the most highly educated graduates who remained in France continued to favor traditional career paths. Although French youth in particular had shown a growing interest in creating start-ups of their own, a survey conducted in January 2000 among workers age 18 to 40 nonetheless found that they continued to value traditional careers. Almost half of all respondents (47 percent) said they would prefer to work in the public than in the private sector. Of the narrow majority who indicated a preference for the private sector (51 percent), four-fifths said they would prefer to work in a "classic" company.[10] This preference for pursuing a professional career with an established employer was strongly felt. More than just providing a stable source of income, France's largest employers—including the largest by far, the state—offered a position of status in French society. The link between career and status had deep roots. In a 1949 article on the French entrepreneurial deficit, David Landes wrote: "Considerations of status . . . were strengthened by such factors as the security of official or professional position and the character of the French educational system, a primary force for social conservatism. For these reasons, the best talents in France almost invariably turned to the traditional honorific careers such as law, medicine, or government. This was true even of the children of businessmen."[11]

For most of the postwar period, France's highly trained elites had been ushered from elite schools into secure positions in the research and development departments of established industrial firms. The Jospin government spent considerable political capital on changing this, by creating incentives for France's technically skilled workers to take on the risk of creating new start-ups in the high-technology sectors. One of its principal tools was the stock option, and it became the focus of an intense political debate over risk and the compensation necessary to promote risk-taking. What emerged from this political process was a complex but broadly favorable regulatory and tax treatment of stock options in France.

Jospin's was not the first effort to encourage the creation of new companies. But earlier efforts had focused primarily on the unemployed. One prominent program, called Aid to Unemployed Founders of Companies (Aide aux chômeurs créateurs ou repreneurs d'entreprises, ACCRE), granted a special exoneration from social security payments to the formerly unemployed who chose to start their own businesses. The program, started in 1984, was reformed six times in ten years. At its inception, ACCRE had offered up to 6,000 euros for any unemployed worker wishing to create a new firm, and it had had a noticeable impact on firm creation. In a 2000 survey of new company owners, 36.2 percent reported having been unemployed before they created a new company.[12] The program was reduced sharply by the Juppé government, then reduced further under Jospin. ACCRE funds were first restricted to certain classes of unemployed.[13] In 1998, Jospin reduced the exemption from social contributions under ACCRE to a single year. These changes caused demand for the program to fall, from 87,000 applicants in 1985 to 34,000 in 1997. The move away from ACCRE was partly a cost-saving measure. The Juppé reforms to ACCRE had netted an estimated 300 million euros. But the government also increasingly saw ACCRE as an inefficient way to encourage new company formation.[14] Especially in new technology sectors, entrepreneurship appeared to require a high level of skill and expertise. One survey of French entrepreneurs, for example, found that 59 percent had previously held upper management positions, and 52 percent had already been company directors.[15]

France's new focus on high-tech start-ups therefore shifted to a strategy of cultivating entrepreneurship among France's most technically skilled workers: those who would normally take top jobs either in government labs or in France's largest and most prestigious companies. In principle, the companies they created would, in turn, create more jobs for the unemployed.

The Stock-Options Debate

The Jospin government hoped to lure the technically skilled out of safe government or industry positions by providing the possibility for attractive compensation to offset the risks of entrepreneurship. The primary strategy for doing so focused on reforming the regulation, and especially the tax treatment, of stock options. Although stock options had existed as a legal financial instrument in France since 1970, the first employee option plans were not created until 1984.[16] Their popularity boomed in 1987, with the support of Edouard Balladur, finance minister under Jacques Chirac and a strong proponent of stock options. Balladur had created a favorable tax status for stock options and removed a ceiling on the number of options any individual employee was permitted to receive, opening the way for stock-option use as a component of executive compensation.[17] In 1990, stock options were further liberalized to extend their application to nontraded companies.[18]

But the trend toward stock option liberalization ended in 1995, when Jean Artuis, minister of finance under Alain Juppé, substantially raised the tax on stock-option earnings. Responding to criticisms that stock options were simply a tool to avoid paying income tax, Artuis raised taxes on stock options from the low level applied to capital earnings (19.4 percent, with no social charges) to 33.4 percent.[19] Artuis's tax rate increase coincided with a study by Andersen Consulting that found that half of all companies in France with more than 2,000 employees used stock options, with over 50,000 managers participating in stock-option plans.[20] It also followed the 1994 revelation through a judicial inquiry that Pierre Suard, CEO of Alcatel-Alsthom, was earning over 2 million euros annually, including 20,000 options on Alcatel-Alsthom stock, a stunning amount for a French executive at the time.[21]

In January 1997, Alain Juppé increased the social contributions due on stock options, raising to 40 percent the total tax on capital gains on stock options held more than five years, and retaining a 54 percent tax (the top marginal income tax rate) on those exercised before five years.[22] This move reflected a genuine concern that corporate management was using stock options to evade taxes.[23] But it meant that, between company and individual contributions, the effective tax rate on stock options could rise to 110 percent.[24] And critically, because the provision was applied retroactively, it proved devastating for technology start-ups that had already begun using stock options as high-powered compensation for their employees. MultiMania, for example, France's first Internet start-up, was forced to eliminate its existing stock-option plan until a more favorable tax treatment appeared.[25] Indeed it was concern over this shift in policy that led leaders in the venture capital and start-up community to create a start-up lobbying organization, Croissance Plus.

The government of Lionel Jospin reversed the trend toward penalizing stock options. Responding in part to the brain drain scare, in part to concerns over France's slow rate of new company formation, Jospin's finance minister and longtime advocate of high technology, Dominique Strauss-Kahn, proposed in January 1999 to lower the tax rate on stock options to 26 percent, equal to the standard tax rate for all capital gains in France. He also proposed to reduce the mandatory holding period required to receive this favorable tax treatment from five years to three years. Management abuses were to be limited through transparency: companies would be required to list managers receiving stock-option packages so that shareholders could monitor their levels of compensation.[26] These provisions were intended to accompany the 1998 law on research and innovation.[27]

French companies had by that time become avid users of stock options. In 1999 the forty largest companies traded on the French *bourse* (CAC40) reported 34,000 stock-option plan holders; thirty-six of these companies reported distributing a total of 67 million options in 1999. This represented a sixfold increase over the number of options distributed in 1993. CAC40 company employees exercised 2.6 billion euros worth of stock options in 1999, up from only 0.6 billion euros in 1998. These figures made France the second largest user of stock options in the world, trailing only the United States.[28] A year 2000 survey of management compensation conducted by the Déminor consulting firm found that 93 percent of France's CAC40 companies offer stock-option plans, compared with only 39 percent of DAX30 companies in Germany and 45 percent of FT30 companies in the UK.[29]

Yet despite their wide use, stock options remained politically controversial in France, and their growing role as a component of compensation for France's top executives proved a sensitive topic. Stock-option packages to management were not reported in the annual reports of large companies, and France's corporate management had been hesitant to reveal their stock-option packages voluntarily. So sensitive was the issue that when Strauss-Kahn proposed to cut taxes on stock-options earnings,

France's largest employer association, Medef, opposed the legislation because of the accompanying transparency requirements.[30] Apparently justifying Medef's concerns, stock options soon became a focus of intensive public condemnation. In September 1999, Elf-Acquitaine revealed that its former CEO, Philippe Jaffré, already the highest paid French executive according to a *Forbes* ranking, had received a severance package that included approximately 24 million euros in stock options.[31] The large amount of money involved took the French population by surprise.

The Jaffré affair created a public backlash against high management compensation in general and against a low tax rate for stock-option earnings in particular. But Strauss-Kahn's plans for lowering the tax rate on general stock options were unlikely to have passed even without Jaffré. At an interministerial meeting on January 7, 1999, Lionel Jospin met with Claude Allègre and Dominique Strauss-Kahn and reportedly came to a decision to back away from the stock-option reform project.[32] This did not put an end to the issue. Later that year, on October 5, the Socialist president of the National Assembly's commission on finances, Augustin Bonrepaux, proposed what came to be called the "Jaffré amendment" to the Finance Law of 2000 (Loi des finances 2000). Rather than lowering the tax on stock-options earnings, as Strauss-Kahn had advocated, the amendment proposed instead to raise it, from 40 percent to 50 percent for individual earnings above 500,000 francs (76,000 euros). Henri Emmanuelli, Bonrepaux's successor, backed the proposal. "In the name of liberalism, of efficiency and of competition," he wrote, "we promote employee flexibility while criticizing their immobility and their interest in security. Yet at the same time we are creating veritable bunkers for top management."[33] The Jaffré amendment had obviously struck a chord with the French left, and was adopted by the majority of Socialist members of Parliament.[34] In an effort to set the issue aside, the Finance Ministry called for a block on any legislation having to do with stock options.[35]

France's contradictory stance toward stock options, combining widespread use with public condemnation, reflected an underlying ambivalence in French society toward merit-based pay. The problem stemmed in part from the twofold use of stock-option packages. On the one hand, stock options were used to align management interests with those of shareholders. With part of their compensation tied to the value of publicly traded stock, managers would take a personal interest in raising the value of the company. This use of stock options to create management incentives was still regarded with suspicion in France, where standards of liberal corporate governance had only recently begun to be introduced. On the other hand, stock options had proven to be a valuable tool in compensating entrepreneurs for the high risks associated with creating new start-ups, and the Jospin government had invested heavily in policies to promote start-ups. But how could Strauss-Kahn support the start-up function of stock options given the criticism they received as a tool for liberal corporate governance? The solution to this apparent impasse was an unusual dual-track approach to the treatment of stock options that distinguished between options used to compensate those who undertook risky entrepreneurial activities and options used to align management incentives with shareholder interests.

In the expectation that his stock-option reform project might face strong political opposition, Strauss-Kahn had made early plans for a parallel category of compensation instrument. Although nearly identical in function to the traditional stock option, the new instrument was designed with a deliberately confusing name: *Bons de souscription de parts de créateurs d'entreprise* (BSPCE).[36] For most they became known simply as *stock-options à la française*.[37] As conceived in the budget legislation of June 1997, the BSPCEs were highly restrictive in their application: they were available only to companies less than seven years old, with 75 percent individual ownership (excluding venture capital firms or other companies), and were not yet traded on a stock market. Over time their scope was expanded. The July 12, 1999, law on innovation and research extended the BSPCE considerably, and by 2002 they applied to companies up to fifteen years old, the ownership requirement had been reduced to 25 percent, and the scope was extended to companies traded on any of Europe's high-tech stock exchanges (France's own Nouveau Marché, Germany's Neuer Markt, and so forth). The finance law for 2000 extended the BSPCE from its early focus on high-tech sectors to include financial markets and insurance companies.

For entrepreneurs, the BSPCE offered a workable solution for a critical need. But they also fulfilled an important political function. For Stauss-Kahn, they were low-hanging fruit that gave him an early victory. The new technology lobbying group Croissance Plus even gave him an award for the success of the BSPCE initiative. More important, this novel stock-option format allowed the political left and right to come together around a consensus that compensation was acceptable in the context of genuine risk-taking. Politicians could promote the small-firm growth that was critical to job creation, without having to accept as a necessary corollary the unchecked use of stock options as a component of management compensation. Indeed concerns remained about the equity of offering preferential tax treatment to what was seen essentially as a component of executive salaries. In the words of Le Duigou, "These are not even innovative companies!"[38]

Stock Options à la française

The logjam was released in part by French appointment of Laurent Fabius as finance minister. Interested in quickly resolving a set of disputes he had not started, Fabius agreed in April 2000 to a multirate compromise that has proved complex but politically successful. Fabius's new tax regime for stock options, which took effect on April 27, 2000, created three tax rates and five taxation categories.[39] The plan set a mandatory four-year holding period. Options exercised before the end of that period are taxed as income, with a top marginal rate of 54 percent. Stocks held for an additional two years face a significantly lower tax rate. In addition, plan holders who earned more than 200,000 euros from options in a year faced higher tax rates than those who earned less (see table 2-1).

Criticized for its complexity, the solution nonetheless responded to two sets of objections that had been raised within the left against stock options. One concern focused on the use of stock options simply as a device for evading income tax. The four-year threshold for exercising options and the two-year delay for selling the stocks represent an effort to limit the use of stock options as a risk-free form of tax-evading compensation. This concern also motivated the elimination of discount options, since these were widely considered to insulate bearers from risk.[40] A second concern was that stock options were being used to conceal high, presumably unjustifiably high, executive compensation packages, since stock options were not reported as compensation on corporate balance sheets. This

Table 2-1.   *Tax Rates for Stock-Option Plans in France*

Percent

Plan type	Years from grant date to sale		
	Less than four years	Four to six years	More than six years
Less than 1 million francs	54[a]	40	26
More than 1 million francs	54[a]	50	40
BSPCE[b]	40	26	26

a. Options held for less than four years are taxed as income, typically at the top marginal rate of 54 percent.

b. *Bons de souscription de parts de créateurs d'entreprise*, available to firms less than fifteen years old.

was the rationale behind the 200,000 euro tax threshold, and the reason that the April 2000 legislation required companies to reveal the stock-option packages of their top ten managers.

The widespread use of both traditional stock options and BSPCEs in France was slowly changing French attitudes toward performance-based compensation, not only among management but also within the labor unions. Since the scandal surrounding the revelation of Jaffré's severance package, and in the shadow of a government legislative project to require that all stock packages be published, prominent French business leaders began revealing their stock-option packages. Jean-Marie Messier, ostentatious CEO of Vivendi Universal, announced in his autobiographical book *J6M* that his 1999 compensation package included stock options totaling 23 million euros. Erneste Sellière, president of France's largest employer association, Medef, announced in 2000 that he had stock options valued at 1.7 million euros.[41]

This new openness reflected a broader change in French attitudes toward risk and compensation. France's Communist trade union, the CGT, for example, supported offering stock options to all employees. Edouard Balladur called for stock options to be offered to all salaried employees. And there appeared to be good reasons for management to consider adopting such a proposal. In 1999, employees at Société Générale had used their 10 percent ownership of the company to block a hostile takeover from Banque Nationale de Paris.[42] Indeed the French telecommunications giant Alcatel was considering offering stock options to all of its 120,000 employees.[43]

Stock options were also becoming increasingly popular among the general public in France. Philippe Jaffré, who first brought stock options into the public debate, invested 150,000 euros to create the website stock-option.fr. The site reported on the uses and advantages of stock-option plans in France and advocated reform of their legal and tax treatment.[44] In January 2001 all French stock options were estimated to have a value of 7.97 billion euros, or roughly 212,000 euros for each of the 37,600 stock-option plan holders.[45] A 2000 study by Ifop found that 80 percent of the French public thought companies should offer stock options to their employees. Interestingly, the same survey found that support for stock options among deputies of the National Assembly was considerably lower, at only 68 percent.[46] It suggests that France's political leaders—who, incidentally, were less likely to benefit from stock-option plans—were out of touch with France's changing attitudes toward performance-based compensation. The reality was that France had come to a political accommodation around the idea that real economic risk-taking should be compensated highly and taxed minimally.

Administrative Reforms

France had long been criticized for bureaucratic excess, and this was increasingly seen as a problem for new company formation. A 1999 survey attributed to France the highest level of administrative regulation among the countries of the Organization for Economic Cooperation and Development (OECD) and the second highest barriers to entrepreneurship, behind only Italy.[47] The cost of creating a new company in France in 1997 was between 1,900 and 4,600 euros, but only 420 euros in Britain and 200–800 euros in the United States.[48] A 1999 business survey found that it took fifteen weeks to register a new company in France, compared with eight weeks in Germany, four weeks in Britain, and only two weeks in the United States.[49] And the burden of government regulation in France was not limited to new firms. In a 2000 survey of heads of small and medium-sized enterprises (SMEs), 21 percent reported that the French government was the greatest constraint on their business performance—greater even than difficulties gaining access to finance (13 percent) or to skilled labor (8 percent). Concern about the government's negative impact on performance was also higher among SMEs in France than in Britain (11 percent), and even slightly higher than in Germany (20 percent).[50] Some of the harshest critics of French regulatory excess were the French themselves, especially those who had moved their companies abroad in search of a friendly working environment. Olivier Cadic, an early and outspoken expatriate entrepreneur who operated a computer-aided design company in Britain, observed, "In France, I was persecuted by [legal] texts and by the bureaucracy. Here, I am free."[51]

Partly in response to such criticisms, the French government focused on lowering administrative barriers to new firm creation. These reforms took two forms. The first and more ambitious was to lower the administrative burden on companies interacting with the French government. In the words of Strauss-Kahn, "The heads of companies are not there to fill out forms, but to produce."[52] But this effort focused less on deregulation, and more on creating a single access point, or *guichet unique*, for business interaction with the government. The Internet and e-government facilities proved especially attractive for implementing the *guichet unique* strategy. A second reform, likely to have a profound long-term impact on French firms, was the introduction into French company law of a new flexible company type, the simplified stock company, whose form derived from the common law tradition of Britain and the United States.

The Guichet Unique

One of the greatest burdens faced by French companies was submitting reports to the government on the status of their business and work force. France had just over 1 million incorporated businesses, and they submitted an estimated 130 million separate reports to the government each year. Of these, 90 percent were due to a dozen mandatory labor- and welfare-related declarations.[53] This burden of paperwork, what the French call *la paperasserie*, fell disproportionately on small employers without specialized accounting departments. It was also perceived to pose a high burden on the heads of companies. In a 1998 survey of salaried employees about their interest in creating their own company, a majority of respondents ranked paying taxes and social contributions as the most challenging task facing the head of a French company, and general government *paperasserie* as the third most challenging task; dealing with competitors came in second.[54] Not only was the administrative burden of running a new company seen as an impediment to entrepreneurs, it also appeared to be depressing hiring among small start-up firms. A report commissioned by the prime minister, released in January 2000, found that 80 percent of newly created companies in France had no employees. It attributed this apparent reluctance to hire partly to the administrative complexities associated with hiring the first employee.[55] In 1996 the Commission Turbot on the simplification of the French pay slip found for example that the French form included twenty-six entries, consisting of a variety of government taxes and withholdings for social programs; its British counterpart included only ten entries.[56]

The government did undertake some small measures to reduce the number of reports that had to be filled out, especially for new start-ups. In June 1999, Lionel Jospin put in place the Commission for Administrative Simplification, or COSA (Commission pour les simplifications administratives). The group had the goal of reducing the administrative burden faced by French companies. Taking on a set of initiatives promoted by Jean-Pierre Raffarin in the former Juppé government, COSA announced thirty-seven measures to simplify company administration. Under this plan, several forms of company reporting would be eliminated. In particular, small firms, those with fewer than ten employees, would move from a monthly to a trimester declaration of employee status. But these reforms were relatively modest, especially when measured against the extensive bureaucratic requirements imposed on French companies.

The French government emphasized instead the goal of streamlining business interaction with the government bureaucracy. The effort especially targeted burdens on new company formation. Coming into office in 1997, Lionel Jospin called for a set of regional offices across France to consolidate all of the procedures for registering a new company. The way for this effort had been paved in January 1994 by the Initiative and Individual Enterprise Law of Alain Madelin, minister of small enterprise in the Balladur administration. This law created among other things a set of Centers for Company Procedures (Centres de formalités des entreprises,

CFEs).[57] Located in regional chambers of commerce and tax centers, the CFEs were designed to centralize advice and paperwork about French companies. The Jospin government pushed to make these centers into *guichets uniques*, or single access points that provided all application forms and information necessary to create or modify a legal corporation. As a part of this measure, Jospin called for companies to be registered rapidly. In some CFEs, company registration took only twenty-four hours.[58]

The French government also aggressively embraced the Internet. By putting services online, it hoped to ease the administrative burden on companies and individuals. The government Internet site, www.admifrance. gouv.fr, made almost all government forms and information available online (later the site became www.service-publique.fr). And French citizens moved quickly to take advantage of this newly convenient access to their government. From 1998 to 1999, visits to the central government website grew fivefold. In 1999, 1 million car registrations (*cartes grises*) were requested over the Internet.[59] Beginning in January 2000, French workers could declare and pay income tax at the site of the Finance Ministry. The government also pushed for a "*dematérialisation*" of new company applications such that they could be submitted in electronic format.[60] By the end of 2000, fully 20 percent of new company creation was occurring through electronic means.[61] Employers' associations, including the top association Medef, the artisans' group Union professionelle artisanale (UPA), and the small-business association Confédération générale des petites et moyennes enterprises (CGPME), all looked favorably upon this simplification.[62]

These rapid advances put France at the leading edge among advanced industrial countries in implementing e-government. Just how advanced is hard to estimate. Comparative measures of e-government penetration were new at the time, and surveys that were conducted tended to be politically motivated and thus unreliable. (When the European Union designed its e-government benchmarking survey, for example, indicators for measuring e-government were proposed by the member states themselves, with each focusing on measures that would show them in a good light.)[63] Nonetheless, French progress appears to have been good. An April 2000 survey by the British government found France on track to be the first government to place all of its services on line.[64] By June 2000, one-third of all

French government services were accessible in an interactive format over the Internet; at the same time in the United States only an estimated 8 percent of all government services were online.[65] In 2002, the French government's document site legifrance.gouv.fr was the largest free public database in the world.[66] One reason e-government was pursued with such enthusiasm was that it allowed the Jospin government to ease the administrative burden on new companies at a relatively low cost and without instituting a bureaucratically painful and politically difficult program of deregulation.

A New Kind of Company

The most common legal forms of companies in France are the Société anonyme (SA) and the Société a responsabilité limité (SARL). For both legal forms, government regulation sets the precise relationship between owners and managers, as well as the relationships among different classes of shareholders, and defines clearly the rights and responsibilities of all. Because most new companies in the mid-1990s were being formed as limited-liability SARLs, the government began by lowering the costs of creating new companies of this kind. Under Jospin, the statutory 10,000 euro initiation fee for the SARL could be distributed over the first five years of a company's existence.[67] Also, social payments by new SARLs were reduced by 30 percent during the first year and by 15 percent during the second year of operation. Despite these new advantages, however, the SARL (and the related EURL, Entreprise unipersonelle à responsabilité limitée) corporate form restricted the ways in which investors and managers could interact. In particular, they limited the control of shareholders over management. While favored by management, this kind of separation had been seen as damaging to new high-technology start-ups, whose potential creditors, in particular venture capitalists, usually decided to invest only if they could also contribute to the direction and management of the new company.

With this in mind, the Jospin administration created a special new legal form for high-tech start-ups that had the potential to revolutionize governance in these sectors. It was based on the Société par action simplifié (SAS). This form of joint-stock company had itself been created recently, in January 1994, in order to provide established companies with a flexible framework for undertaking collaborative projects.[68] Before the SAS, French companies seeking to create joint stock companies moved abroad in Europe. Many went to the Netherlands, where corporate law had traditionally been more flexible.[69] As originally conceived, the SAS was restricted to companies possessing a capitalization of at least 230,000 euros, and could only be created by an existing corporation. This effectively limited its usefulness to relatively large companies. In July 1999, in a move that some felt might reshape the landscape of French corporate governance, the Law on Innovation and Research created a variant of the SAS that could be formed by an individual entrepreneur.[70]

This new company form had first been advocated by Philippe Pouletty, French owner of the Silicon Valley firm SangStat and head of Objectif 2010, a lobbying group with the ambitious goal of making France the premier creator of innovative companies by 2010.[71] At a meeting held in December 1998 between French entrepreneurs from Silicon Valley and thousands of students from France's elite schools, Pouletty called on Strauss-Kahn to create a new liberal company format.[72] Strauss-Kahn's response was optimistic: "Why not create a new business statute for companies of the new economy? We must reconcile the French to risk."[73] Although the law was originally intended to support only high-tech companies, legislators were unable to set objective innovative criteria, so they broadened it to include all economic sectors. It was incorporated at the last minute in the 1999 law on innovation. The Paris Chamber of Commerce and Industry observed: "It is certainly regrettable that such an important reform has resulted from an amendment adopted at the edge of the discussion of a law focused in principle on innovation and on research."[74]

The newly expanded SAS was, like its predecessor, limited to privately owned companies. Companies employing this corporate form could therefore not issue stock publicly. But aside from this limitation, the SAS seemed to offer several advantages. It permitted companies to create their own rules for management and stockholders.[75] This allowed different classes of shares to be granted different voting rights, a condition that was considered necessary to attract first- and second-round venture capital. Furthermore, the new SAS format allowed new start-ups to issue stock options, something not permitted under the SARL format, and allowed the board of directors to make decisions via phone or e-mail rather than in face-to-face meetings, as required by the SARL.[76] Finally, French companies had been required since 1981 to form works councils when workers requested them. While recommendations of the works councils were not binding, they were required to meet once a year with management. One effect of the new SAS format would be to eliminate the already weak role of works councils in company management. For all of these reasons, the new SAS was greeted as a boon to innovative start-ups.

But while the new SAS company form would in principle allow small start-ups to structure company management with a high level of flexibility, its early years highlighted the challenges of importing new liberal institutions into a highly regulated economy. Legally the SAS was complex, and in the absence of clear standards of interpretation, that complexity brought uncertainty for the intrepid companies who were the first to use the new form. It was also not available to publicly traded companies. And, at least initially, companies wishing to convert to another company form had to wait for two years.[77] This provision was soon eliminated, but conversion to another company form still required 100 percent support from shareholders. This opened the risk that a single shareholder could block the public flotation of the company.[78] As one of France's leading venture capitalists summarized, "Professional venture capitalists, when they take on new companies, shift them immediately from SAS to SA. The SA is just more secure."[79]

Public Infrastructure for Private Innovation

The French government still played a strong role in setting basic research priorities. The public sector accounted for 40 percent of all research and development undertaken in France at the time and for nearly half of all researchers. French industry employed about 168,000 researchers, the public sector about 155,000.[80] One of the challenges facing France's minister of research, Claude Allègre, was to find a strategy for transferring new basic science discoveries from state-funded laboratories into new technology start-ups.

One of Allègre's early efforts made it easier, and less risky, for researchers in France's publicly funded research organizations, including the public university system and the network of national laboratories (the Centre national de la recherche scientifique, CNRS; the Institute national français de recherche medicale, INSERM; and the Institut national de recherche en informatique et en automatique, INRIA), to commercialize their research findings. The main problem was that public researchers had been legally prohibited from taking a stake in private companies. The 1999 Law on Innovation eliminated this restriction, permitting researchers in government labs, as well as university professors and researchers, to take up to 15 percent ownership in a company.[81] It also permitted employees to take a "company creation holiday" (congé création d'entreprise), granting up to six years' leave of absence, including social security coverage, with a guarantee of receiving one's old job upon return.[82] Under the old system, an estimated twenty government researchers per year had renounced their jobs to create new companies. The Jospin government hoped to push that up to about 100 per year. They referred to this goal as essaimage, a mass movement of researchers away from government research facilities. Although five out of six new companies created by researchers were ultimately successful,[83] the goal of the new policies was to lower the cost for those who failed.

Of course, most entrepreneurs are not scientists. France therefore reorganized its system of national laboratories in order to promote the transfer of technologies out of government research labs and into new start-up companies headed by entrepreneurs. In the past, when technology was transferred from government laboratories to France's large corporations, collaborators had been easy to identify. But with the new emphasis on the small-firm sector as a means of commercializing technology, knowing whom to work with was not so easy. Both Claude Allègre, minister of research and industry under Jospin, and his successor, Roger-Gérard Schwartzenberg, therefore tried to rationalize the system of government research centers in order to create better communication among communities of researchers, entrepreneurs, and industrialists working with similar technologies. Their goal was to place researchers and practitioners in close contact with one another, so that new ideas could cross the boundary from laboratory to industry.

Two different visions of technology transfer drove the French restructuring: the idea of the research network, and the model of the technology park. Rather than deciding between these paradigms, France embraced both. The government planned to create sixteen innovation networks that linked existing researchers with industry, by sector. In addition, existing and new research facilities were grouped by technology area into twelve technology research centers distributed around France. Both approaches were designed to bring together research labs and companies working in related fields of technology.[84] Under this new dual system, private companies worked side-by-side with government-sponsored research labs, including the prestigious CNRS and INRIA.

The network model was embodied in the new Networks for Research and Technological Innovation (Réseaux de recherche et d'innovation technologique, RRIT). By 2002, France had created thirteen of these networks, all in technical fields in which the government believed important commercial advances could be made. Four of the RRITs focus on information and communications technology:

—The National Network for Telecommunications Research (Réseau national de recherche en télécommunications, RNRT) was created in 1998. The 8.7 million euros it distributed in 2000 were divided almost evenly among public labs, large companies, and small companies.

—The National Network for Micro- and Nano-technologies (Réseau de recherche en micro- et nano-technologies, RMNT), created in 1999, focused on microelectronics, optoelectronics, and microstructures.

—The National Network on Software Technology (Réseau national des technologies logicielles, RNTL), created in 2000, had a budget in 2001 of 13 million euros. Of this, 45 percent went to public labs and 55 percent to industry.

—The Network for Research and Innovation in Audiovisual and Multimedia (Réseau audiovisuel et multimédia, RIAM) was created February 21, 2001.[85]

The goal of these networks was to help direct government research funds to worthy projects. France had no history of independent agencies, like the National Science Foundation or the National Institutes of Health in the United States, to distribute research funds. The RRITs were created to play the role of the research branch of such an agency. Thus each RRIT had an advisory board and an executive committee. The executive committee drafted a request for proposals. Outside experts reviewed the proposals and submitted their recommendations to the advisory board. Projects that were approved received a certification from the network, and that certification, or *label*, was recognized by government ministries who disbursed funds.[86] Between 1998 and 2002, the RRITs granted 299 million euros to 820 projects.[87] Of course, problems remained with the new system. The requirement to submit proposals still penalized start-ups, since doing so required significant preparation. And because the network was explicitly French, it discouraged collaboration across borders. Nonetheless, it was greeted by researchers as a significant success.[88]

A second effort emphasized the importance of technology clusters in promoting the skills, infrastructure, and communication that engender technical innovation. Technology parks had a long history in French technology policy. One of the oldest of these, located in a picturesque setting on the Valbonne Plateau above Nice, is Sophia-Antipolis. Founded in 1969 in collaboration with the Ecole des Mines on 200 hectares of land, the site was selected as part of the program to decentralize industrial capacity within France. By 2000, it provided a home to more than 1,100 companies and 25,000 technical and scientific staff.[89] Sophia-Antipolis also includes several incubators, and, although half of Sophia-Antipolis's employees at the time worked in telecommunications sectors, their research focus left them relatively unscathed by the dot.com recession. Indeed from January 2000 to June 2001 they created 3,000 new jobs and thirty-four new companies.[90]

Such early technology parks, called *technopôles,* were typically the site of collaboration between government labs and national champions pursuing major technological projects. Sophia-Antipolis, for example, was at the core of the Ministry of Telecommunications' effort to revitalize the French telecommunications network in the late 1970s. Grenoble, site of another *technopôle*, became the center of France's semiconductor research, in which Thompson collaborated with the government-sponsored EFSIS project (Étude et fabrication de circuits intégrés spéciaux) to develop microelectronics.[91]

In the late 1990s, the traditional *technopôles* were integrated into a new set of National Centers for Technological Research (Centres nationaux de recherche technologique, CNRT). Unlike the research networks, which were virtual, these new CNRTs were intended to promote technologies

Table 2-2.   *National Research and Technology Centers*

Location	Research focus
Belfort, Montbeliard	Fuel cells
Caen	Electronic materials
Evry	Genomics
Grenoble	Micro- and nanotechnologies
Lyon	Chemistry, molecular biology
Marcoussis	Optics, lasers, optoelectronics
Marseille	Energy
Metz, Pont-a-Mousson	Metallurgy
Rennes, Lannion, Brest	Telecommunications
Rouen	Combustion, motors
Sophia-Antipolis	Information technology
Toulouse	Space, aeronautics
Tours	New materials, high-power microelectronics

Source: *Le Monde*, September 11, 2001.

requiring specialized or expensive platform technologies. They also provided a way to balance concerns about regional development in France with the new technology initiatives of the government. But although these centers were pushed by Claude Allègre, little money was allocated to them. Those that succeeded were able to build on preexisting capacities. A new center within Sophia-Antipolis, for example, has been designated the focus for information and communications technology. A newly created center in Evry focuses on genomics. The center in Marcoussis, the Laboratoire de photonique et de nanostructures (LPN), focuses on lasers and opto-electric devices. The long-term plan called for roughly twenty such centers (see table 2-2).

These two technology transfer systems were not entirely separate, because research centers (CNRTs) were also often members of the thematic networks (RRITs).[92] Both represented new efforts to permit government-funded labs to promote the commercialization of technology through new start-ups. Indeed one of the greatest challenges facing these reform projects was the shift that the researchers faced, from working with large and highly competent industrial leaders, like France Télécom and Thompson, to working with entrepreneurs in small start-ups. This organization of research labs and companies by technology was new and experimental. Certainly the change had not been easy, and state researchers were "having a hard time leaving behind the culture of the '*grands projets*,'" suggests innovation expert Jacques Martineau.[93] But the new initiatives did help to maximize the interaction between researchers and entrepreneurs. And they allowed the government to define a set of fifteen to twenty technology areas that they felt French start-ups might profitably pursue.

Conclusions

In July 1998, France's Interministerial Council on Research set a goal of creating several hundred stable new technology firms in France over the following four years. Their recommendations for achieving this goal addressed three impediments to the growth of small firms: administrative burdens on new companies, incentives to entrepreneurship, and barriers to technology transfer. Since then, French regulatory reforms have accordingly attempted to reduce these impediments. New provisions for taxing stock options helped to create incentives for entrepreneurs to remain in France. France has also pursued a concerted effort to reduce the burden of administrative reporting and oversight on small companies. Its creation of a new form of company, the SAS, gives start-ups greater flexibility in designing the relationship between management and investors. And France's reorganization of its national research labs encourages greater interaction with the new entrepreneurial class. Most striking about these reforms was what they were not: namely, broad deregulation. The French government did not renounce it traditional role as arbiter of business activity. Nor did it extend provisions for liberal corporate management beyond new start-ups.

But France's new entrepreneurial enthusiasm was also not imposed entirely from above. Part of its impetus clearly came from high rates of unemployment, although these fell (from 12.4 percent in 1997 to 8.4 percent in 2001) during the period in which entrepreneurship was becoming more popular. More important, rapid privatization of large state-owned technology firms was pushing highly skilled engineers into the private sector. Even France's most highly trained technical elite found their traditional career plans blocked by a baby-boomer generation that was holding up promotions in France's large companies. "The royal path is blocked," noted one venture capitalist.[94] As the advantages of the classical career trajectory became less attractive, the entrepreneurial track took on increasing allure.[95]

Whatever its sources, France's move to a new "culture of risk" carried its own risks for the French economy. The success of postwar France both in generating cutting-edge innovation and in amassing extraordinary wealth was premised not on economic liberalism but on a careful coordination of research and industry effort against the political background of wage equality and administrative oversight. The French government under Jospin and Chirac attempted to embrace individual entrepreneurship, but without relinquishing its responsibilities for sustaining France's social contract. Their experiment offers the possibility of generating a new hybrid form of technology innovation, one in which entrepreneurship and social responsibility coexist. Certainly the high levels of education and cultural achievement attained in France should attract rather than discourage entrepreneurs. And in the uncertain job market that start-ups seem to require, strong social supports should be a benefit rather than a liability. But the French solution also has a lot of working parts. The complex regulatory formulas France has erected to encourage entrepreneurship demand, if anything, more rather than less government regulatory oversight. Thus even if it succeeds, the French approach may not be easily accessible to countries with traditions of weaker state participation in the economy.

CHAPTER THREE

Private Equity
in the Shadow
of the State

In March 2000, France's homegrown Internet portal MultiMania made an initial public offering (IPO) on the country's new high-tech stock market, the Nouveau Marché. As the market's first major Internet IPO, the MultiMania launch fired the public imagination. From an initial offering price of 36 euros, the stock was bid up over forty-eight hours to 125 euros. Demand for the retail tranche was 112 times oversubscribed, with 250,000 separate orders. Demand for the professional investor tranche was 70 times oversubscribed. To the press, MultiMania looked like a French analog to the dot-com phenomenon of the United States. Formed in 1996 by Michel Meyer, who had recently returned from Silicon Valley to fulfill his military service, MultiMania was France's first major Internet start-up to succeed through venture capital support. Initial funding came from Sofinnova Partners, with subsequent rounds from Financière des Cinq, Paribas, and Intel Atlantic. BNP Paribas and Merrill Lynch comanaged the IPO, which raised 64 million euros. Through their support, MultiMania had in four years become France's fifth-most-popular website, behind France Télécom's site Wanadoo and the American sites Yahoo, Lycos, and AOL. Perhaps most surprising for France, it had achieved this market share without any public support. In November 2000, Lycos Europe purchased MultiMania in a stock swap worth 222 million euros.[1]

While not uncommon by the standards of the American technology exchange, NASDAQ, the MultiMania flotation nevertheless seemed to mark a revolution in French industry. Major technological innovations that France had achieved during most of the postwar period—from the Concorde to the very successful space program, from Minitel to the TGV— were born of government-sponsored and funded collaboration between France's prestigious government scientific and technical labs and France's large corporations, the so-called national champions. The French state provided funding either directly or through loan guarantees; it was also typically the customer for these products. This approach to R&D amounted to what Jean-Jacques Salomon has described as innovation without risk: "With guaranteed markets for new innovations, producers could afford to take on big technological challenges."[2] In this approach, the risks of development were borne in common, and the fruits of success were shared universally. It created a low-risk environment that promoted research and development projects that were large and cutting-edge, but also slow.

France's innovation landscape began to change in the 1990s. The French government and French banks at the time still provided a large amount of capital to the technology sector: in 1996, government funds accounted for 54 percent of total R&D in France, compared with only 43 percent in the United States and 32 percent in Japan.[3] But France had also begun to encourage private equity investment in order to promote the commercialization of new technologies. The policy shift responded partly to the successes of the U.S. venture capital model, which had driven dramatic successes in computers and software. It also reflected the reality that the French state could no longer bear the full fiscal burden of commercializing new technologies. France's new approach, as conceived by Dominique Strauss-Kahn, would be "small, fast, and private."[4] Favorable new tax policies would encourage domestic investors to move into risky venture capital. Late-stage private equity, including buyout and restructuring funds, would help prepare new companies for flotation. And the Nouveau Marché, Europe's first technology stock exchange, would provide an exit strategy for these early investors. In 1999, France led Europe in initial public offerings with fifty-five (in that year there were fifty in Germany, thirty-six in England).[5]

Figure 3-1.   *Early- and Late-Stage Private Equity Invested in France,*
1992–2002

Billions of euros

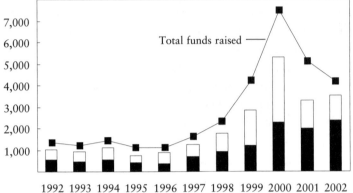

■ Invested in late stage □ Invested in early stage (VC)

Source: PricewaterhouseCoopers, "Rapport sur l'Activité du Capital-investissement en France, 2001"
(Paris: Association Française des investisseurs en capital, 2002), p. 32; PricewaterhouseCoopers, *Les chiffres*
2002 du capital investissement (Paris: AFIC, 2003); European Venture Capital Association, *EVCA Year-*
book (Brussels: EVCA, various years).

By 2000, it appeared that France's new initiatives were succeeding.
Despite signs of a looming technology sector decline, France raised 7.5
billion euros in private equity investment that year (see figure 3-1). Of
this, 57 percent went to venture capital funds. This represented a 75 percent increase over 1999, when 4.28 billion euros were raised. By the end
of 2000, the total stock of private equity invested in France, including
both early- and late-stage investment, amounted to 15.9 billion euros,
making France the third largest market for private equity investment in
the world, behind Britain, with 17 billion euros, and the United States,
with 100 billion euros. Of course, French investment in technology tended
to follow the boom-bust cycle experienced in the technology sectors of all
advanced industrial economies over this period. As a proportion of all private equity investment, the high-technology sectors grew from 29 percent in
1999 to 45 percent in 2000, then fell to 22.6 percent in 2001.[6] Venture
capital funds invested in Internet start-ups raised 400 million euros in 1999,
almost twice the year before, and a further 1 billion euros in 2000, then fell
to 800 million euros in 2001.[7] These declines notwithstanding, France had
in a short period developed a functioning venture capital community and a
strong field of new technology start-ups.

France's move to cultivate private sources of risk investment, however, did not mean that the government was stepping back from its traditional role in setting technology policy. We observe instead a dual motion, toward greater private investment *and* greater government involvement. While France appeared to have accepted the need to promote private sources of funding for developing and commercializing new technology, it did not necessarily agree that private investors would make more rational allocation decisions than the state could. Government incentives for private investment in new technologies provided guidance—partly through active tax policies and partly through administrative oversight—concerning what kinds of firms and technologies to support. And the Jospin administration did not believe that individual investors were necessarily best suited to judge their own level of acceptable risk. It attempted instead to limit individual exposure by placing ceilings on tax incentives for risky investments. Thus, while France was willing to tap France's high level of private savings in order to promote the new economy, it was still reluctant to leave to individual investors decisions that would have broader economic or distributional ramifications.

Venture Capital without Capitalists

In the United States and in Britain, risky ventures were disproportionately financed by pension funds and affluent private individuals. Both of these classes of investors controlled sufficiently large pools of capital to diversify the high risk associated with private equity investment. Distinctive features of France's political economy would force it to look elsewhere for sources of private risk investment.

A first obstacle to promoting private equity in France was the virtual absence of domestic private pension funds. U.S. venture capitalists at the time raised over half of their capital from private pension funds. European countries such as Britain and Sweden also had large pension funds that invested heavily in risky start-ups. Pension funds contributed 35 percent of new Swedish private equity in 2000, and 40 percent of new British private equity.[8] The large volume of capital these large funds held allowed them to diversify the high risks associated with new technology companies.

In France, however, private pension funds were widely perceived to threaten the country's popular pay-as-you-go pension system.[9] Retiring French workers received 70 percent of their working wage in pension payments through the public system. This compared with only 17 percent for the British pension system and 37 percent in the United States.[10] The French system's generosity made it popular and thus difficult for politicians to reform. When Prime Minister Alain Juppé had attempted to reform the public sector pension system in 1995, for example, 2 million public employees took to the streets of Paris to protest. Eventually France's pension system would have to be reformed—Germany had already undertaken painful changes—and any solution was likely to give a role to private pension funds. But the Jospin government, apparently taking note of Juppé's experience, backed away from any pension reform efforts, leaving French venture capitalists to seek other sources of funding.

A second obstacle concerned the tax treatment of potential private equity investors. The problem was that French tax law penalized not just capital gains, as in other countries, but also wealth. France's wealth solidarity tax (impôt de solidarité sur la fortune, ISF) was first applied in 1982, under the Socialist government of François Mitterrand. The ISF was an annual tax, starting at 0.55 percent, on all individually held wealth above 4.7 million francs. In 2000 it touched about 170,000 households.[11] For individuals who owned large stakes in companies, the wealth solidarity tax could increase their effective tax rate up to a ceiling of 85 percent of their income![12] This tax could be particularly onerous for individual investors who took significant stakes in new start-ups. "All of the 'business angels' are packing their bags because they don't want to pay the ISF," commented Antoine Décitre, cofounder of the Paris-based business incubator Tocamak.[13] Interestingly, despite concerns about lagging entrepreneurship, the government would not touch the ISF. The Economics Ministry briefly considered a proposal to exempt all equity holdings from the ISF. There was a strong precedent for such an exemption. Jack Lang, minister of culture in the Mitterrand administration, had exempted works of art held by private individuals from the wealth tax. And both the Senate and the National Assembly had shown interest in ISF reform.[14] But politically, such a move was impossible. As one former Economics Ministry official described the challenge, "For the left, touching ISF is worse than pedophilia."[15] In 1999 the top marginal rate for the wealth tax was actually increased to 1.8 percent per year for fortunes above 15 million euros.

Enticing Private Investors

In an effort to tap France's high savings rate to promote technological innovation, the Juppé government in 1996 proposed tax incentives for ordinary French households to invest in venture capital. François d'Aubert, secretary of state for research under Juppé, was one of the first to call for greater individual investment in corporate innovation. Since 1983, France had offered tax incentives for sophisticated private individuals to undertake risky early-stage investments. This early provision, called the Fonds communs de placement à risques (FCPR), had become the foundation of a successful but small early venture capital community in France. To widen the source of VC funds, d'Aubert's plan was to extend the benefits of the FCPR to less-knowledgeable investors in the broad public. He proposed the creation of a powerful new investment tax incentive, what he called "mutual funds invested in innovation" (Fonds communs de placement dans l'innovation, FCPI). The project was implemented under Strauss-Kahn beginning in 1997.

FCPIs offered tax advantages for individual investors who placed their funds in highly innovative firms. These funds, run by private fund managers, were required to invest 60 percent of their capital in medium-sized firms focused on innovation that were either not publicly listed or listed on France's high-tech stock market, the Nouveau Marché. The terms of the FCPI were fiscally attractive, but restrictive. If the FCPI was held for five years, earnings and value added were exempt from tax, although they were susceptible to the 10 percent social contribution.[16] In order to keep the tax incentives from disproportionately subsidizing the wealthy, investors received this deduction only up to 75,000 francs (11,433 euros) invested annually or 150,000 francs (22,867 euros) per married couple.[17] Furthermore, 90 percent of funds had to be invested within a two-year period, limiting the amount of time for fund managers to evaluate potential projects.

To qualify for these tax exemptions, target companies had to show that they were "intensively innovative," and this could be accomplished in one of two ways. First, any firm was eligible for FCPI funds if it had spent at least one-third of its revenue over three consecutive years on research and development activities. Of course, most new innovative firms had not been in existence long enough to meet this test. Alternatively, young start-ups that did not yet have an R&D track record were nonetheless eligible for FCPI funding if they received certification from the state innovation agency, ANVAR (Agence nationale pour la valorisation de la recherche). By June of 2001, ANVAR had certified 380 innovative companies as intensively innovative.[18] In practice, almost all companies that received FCPI funds had also been approved by ANVAR.[19] In this way France's tax code made ANVAR a sort of gatekeeper for private funding to new innovative companies.

ANVAR had been created under de Gaulle in 1967 as a means for commercializing the research results of France's network of state-sponsored research labs, the National Center for Scientific Research (CNRS). Its mission was broadened in 1979 under the government of Raymond Barre to include the promotion of innovation in private industry. As part of this shift, ANVAR began to invest at a zero percent interest rate in industry research projects that were likely to yield commercially applicable technologies. It was repaid only if the project succeeded. In 1986, Prime Minister Jacques Chirac reduced ANVAR's budget and restricted its activities to funding innovation in France's small and medium-sized enterprises, those with fewer than 2,000 employees.[20]

Renamed the Agence française de l'innovation (but still called ANVAR), ANVAR in 2000 had twenty-five regional delegations with a total of 280 investigators. It also drew on a network of 1,700 external experts to help evaluate the innovation potential of new projects, and dispensed approximately 215 million euros annually to new research projects.[21] Two-thirds of those funds came from government appropriations and one-third from the repayment of outstanding loans. By the late 1990s, biotechnology had become a major target of ANVAR support, with about 27 percent of its funds focused on this area. ANVAR also directed an increasing portion of its support to new information and communications technologies (NICTs). Between 1998 and 2000, ANVAR support for NICTs doubled, from 15 percent of total investments to 31 percent.[22] Part of this growth was due to ANVAR's decision in 2000 to support innovation not only in manufacturing but also in services, especially Internet service companies. Internet grants accounted for 8 percent of the year 2000 budget, and doubled in 2001 to 15 percent of the budget. ANVAR was also increasingly focused on funding new start-ups. In 2001, companies less than three years old accounted for 41 percent of ANVAR's budget.[23]

There is little question that ANVAR was an influential force in cultivating small-firm-based technology in France. Of all high-tech start-ups created in France between 1987 and 1999, 84 percent had enjoyed ANVAR support. And ANVAR had a surprisingly good record of picking winners: 70 percent of companies created with ANVAR support stayed in business for at least ten years, and 55 to 60 percent of the loans issued by ANVAR were repaid. ANVAR had also earned a good reputation among venture capital managers, who increasingly took their cues from ANVAR in making their own investment decisions, even outside of the FCPI tax framework. Philippe Méré, director of Banexi Ventures Partners, one of France's new venture capital funds, reported, "Almost all of the innovative SMEs we have financed had been supported by an ANVAR project."[24]

ANVAR's new role in certifying companies for the FCPI also gradually changed their organizational priorities, leading them to take on many of the functions that had traditionally been provided by private venture capitalists. In 1997, ANVAR amended its charter to include a headhunter function, recruiting technical and scientific experts for the PMEs it supported. In 1998, ANVAR adopted a policy to leverage its limited funds by encouraging private investment alongside its own grants. It signed agreements with private venture capital groups: Sofinnova Partners, Technocom Apax Partners, Atlas Venture, Financière Natexis, CDC participations, BNP Private Equity (Banexi), and Spef-Groupe Banques Populaires. In 1999, ANVAR signed additional agreements with ABN Amro, Galileo Partners, and 3i.[25] These agreements had the goal of coordinating public and private sources of investment in order to allocate available investments more rationally. ANVAR also began granting loans to help start-ups prepare for flotation on the Nouveau Marché.[26] Finally, in January 2002, ANVAR extended its support from single projects to entire companies and began to take stock options in those companies as compensation.[27] Increasingly, ANVAR came to be seen as a public business angel.[28]

Not everyone was happy about ANVAR's extended mandate. First, the organization suffered from bureaucratic excess. As one former Jospin official said of ANVAR, "It is a very dynamic [organization], from a Soviet perspective." Entrepreneurs who interacted with ANVAR confirmed this view. "It was like Kafka," reported Fabrice Cavarretta, founder of the Internet start-up Ipropi.fr; "Getting through it required psychological support."[29] MultiMania approached ANVAR for support, but balked at the volume of paperwork.[30] Second, ANVAR was a target for government and business pressure in evaluating the innovativeness of new start-ups. FCPI fund managers, for example, reportedly lobbied for ANVAR support for projects they wanted to fund, although there is no evidence that this influenced ANVAR's evaluation.[31] And in 1999 the prime minister's office reportedly asked ANVAR to soften its standards for awarding innovation certificates so that FCPI fund managers could invest in more secure later-stage companies. Despite such challenges, most French venture capitalists praised ANVAR: for the strong scientific expertise it provided, for contracting out much of its technical work, for the quality of its financial advice, and for the additional funds it offered to supplement support from private venture capital. In the absence of a strong VC culture in France, ANVAR seemed to provide the missing technical expertise.

The FCPIs for which ANVAR provided certification enjoyed success among investors. These funds were managed by France's large banks and insurance companies, including Axa Placement Innovation and Société Générale.[32] In the first year they were available, 1997, FCPIs raised 61 million euros.[33] They raised an additional 370 million euros in 2000, and 500 million euros in 2001, bringing the total raised by June 2001 to 1.5 billion euros.[34] On the basis of these early signs of success, Laurent Fabius announced in December 2000 that he would extend the FCPI tax exemption for an additional five years, until 2006.[35] And in response to concerns expressed by the European Union, the FCPI exemption would be made available beginning in 2003 to investment in any qualifying European start-up (although not to European start-ups taken over by American owners).

In addition to the private funds it raised, the FCPI program sponsored an entirely new generation of venture capital fund managers. Many were recruited from consulting firms such as Accenture. Société Générale, for example, staffed its FCPI fund with experts from the Finance Ministry. Teams that began young and inexperienced quickly learned the skills of venture capital, although often the hard way.[36] And by allowing individual households to invest more directly in new ventures, the FCPI cut out several layers of financial intermediaries.

But the FCPI program also raised concerns among professional VC fund managers. It employed a powerful tax incentive to induce middle-class households to invest in extremely risky ventures. Restrictions placed on FPCIs to limit that risk also made them complicated investment tools to manage. Caps were placed not only on the size of individual investments but also on the percentage of any fund that could be invested in a single company. No individual fund could invest more than 15 percent of its total shares in one company, and only 60 percent of any fund could be allocated to high-tech start-ups. These provisions could lead to erratic investment decisions. As new shares were bought and sold, for example, fund managers could be forced to buy and sell shares in companies in which they had already invested so as to comply with the 15 and 60 percent caps.[37]

More significantly, experienced VC fund managers worried that the high levels of risk that the new investors were taking on could spoil the opportunity to widen the future base of private equity investors.[38] Venture capital is a patient person's game, but the bulk of FCPI funds were required by law to be invested within two years of being raised. Traditional venture capitalists worried that the speed of FCPI investment, coupled with the inexperience of many of the fund managers, would lead some funds to make bad choices. One analyst suggested that FCPI funds might return only 40 percent of their value! Experienced FCPI teams, such as Axa Placement Innovation, recognized this problem, and began moving their FCPI investments toward lower-risk service sector start-ups in order to offset the risks created by the need to invest rapidly.

Institutional Investors

With individual investors still new to venture capital, the bulk of French private equity came from traditional institutional investors (see table 3-1). Institutional investors were often derided in French public discourse for

Table 3-1. *Sources of Private Equity Funds by Country, 2000*
Percent

Source	France	Germany	Sweden	United Kingdom
Individuals	5	11	7	6
Pension funds	17	6	35	40
Corporations	13	9	2	8
Banks	39	29	11	10
Insurance	9	16.4	12	15
Government	2	16	3	4

Source: European Venture Capital Association, *EVCA Yearbook 2000* (Brussels: EVCA, 2001).

the power they exercised over company management. Because many were foreign, often "Anglo-Saxon," institutional investors were seen to favor shareholder value over employment security. The highly politicized lay-offs in the spring of 2001 at Danone and Marks and Spencer were blamed in particular on earnings pressure from American pension funds.[39] Despite this polemical apprehension, however, French start-ups still relied heavily on the country's large financial institutions as a source of venture capital. Foreign pension funds alone constituted 17 percent of private equity raised in France in 2000. Taken together, banks, insurance, pension funds, and corporate venturing constituted over two-thirds of all private equity. While the rise of French venture capital appeared to signal a fundamental shift in technology policy, the bulk of new funds came from the same institutions that had supported French innovation in the past.

Perhaps the most obvious place to turn for private equity investment was to France's banks. Banks had always funded French innovation, often through loans guaranteed by the state. And banks still made loans directly to start-ups. A 2000 survey of French start-ups found that 22 percent relied on bank loans for financing, while 24 percent relied on venture capital (the majority of start-ups still relied on personal savings).[40] Such loans were still commonly backed by guarantees from government agencies. Most prominent among banks that offered such guaranteed funding was the state-owned Development Bank for Small and Medium-Sized Enterprises (Banque du Développement des Petites et Moyennes Entreprises, BDPME). Created in January 1997 from a consolidation of two other loan-granting agencies (SOFARIS and the Crédit d'Equipement des PME,

CEPME), the BDPME secured up to 70 percent of the value of loans for start-ups. At the time, nearly half of private bank loans to new start-ups were secured by the BDPME.[41] But commercial banks were also increasingly investing in venture capital funds. Some banks created their own funds. Crédit Agricole, for example, founded Crédit Agricole Création, which took up to a 25 percent stake in start-ups. Indeed the BDPME had itself begun guaranteeing the stake that some venture capital funds took in new start-ups.[42] In 2000, fully 39 percent of all private equity investment came from banks. Some of this included FCPI funds run by banks.

Another attractive source of funds for start-ups was life insurance, which constituted the largest single pool of private savings in France. Thanks to favorable tax treatment, French citizens traditionally invested heavily in life insurance policies. A 1999 survey by the French polling group Sofres found that 40 percent of individual French savings for retirement was invested in these policies.[43] And in 2000, life insurance accounted for 80 percent of new savings.[44] Historically, these investments, amounting to about 30 percent of GDP, supported public debt and private bonds. In the 1990s they also became a logical place for France to look for funding for technology start-ups.

In 1997, Economics Minister Dominique Strauss-Kahn introduced a new form of private life insurance policy that would apply a small part of this savings to investment in new technologies. The eponymous DSK Policies (Contrats DSK) invested at least half of its capital in the French stock market, the *bourse*, and an additional 5 percent in high-tech start-ups—either those already listed on the Nouveau Marché or new companies that were not yet publicly traded. These new insurance policies raised 8.5 billion euros in 1999, 427 million euros of which went to financing innovative projects.[45] They accounted for much of the growth in insurance contributions to private equity, which increased from 12 percent in 1996 to 19 percent in 1999. (This level fell to 9 percent in 2000, apparently on concerns about the likely effects of the U.S. technology bubble.) If DSK policies were well received in France, they attracted negative attention from Brussels. The European Commission criticized their 50 percent French content requirement as an unfair subsidy to French firms, as an obstacle to the free flow of capital, and as a restriction on the free provision of services within the European Union. France responded by extending the risky component of the DSK policies to all European stocks and companies.[46]

A third and increasingly important institutional source of capital for French start-ups came from France's large industrial corporations. Liberalization of French corporate governance and the decline of bank-funded innovation for France's large technology firms forced them to adopt more cost-effective approaches to innovation. Often this simply meant acquiring companies as a means of absorbing new technologies. Vivendi, for example, purchased the American company MP3 in order to acquire its digital compression technology. For truly new technologies or markets, however, French companies increasingly began taking equity stakes in small start-ups, especially those pursuing work in areas related to their own core businesses.

To this end, many of France's large technology firms created their own corporate venture capital funds (see table 3-2). Air Liquide, Schneider, and Pinault-Printemps-Rédoute all created their own venture capital branches.[47] Air Liquide Ventures, for example, pursued new technologies that offered synergies with Air Liquide's line of medical products. The venture group was highly international, with employees from five countries and a second office in Stockholm. It reviewed 700 dossiers per year, and from its creation in November 1999 until the end of 2001 had invested 18 million euros.[48] In addition to financial resources, Air Liquide Ventures brought the start-ups it supported to the negotiating table with its own customers. One supported start-up, Capsule Technology, provided real-time information exchange between pieces of medical equipment. It was scheduled to receive 40 million euros from Air Liquide Ventures over the course of seven years, and when Air Liquide approached its clients, it also advertised the Capsule Technology product.[49]

The fourth important institutional investor in France was, inevitably, the state. In 1998, Economics Minister Dominique Strauss-Kahn, who became known as the "minister of high-tech" for his enthusiasm for new technology sectors, allocated 153 million euros from the sale of France Télécom stock to create a fund of funds that would promote high-tech sectors in France.[50] Indeed one of the arguments for the partial privatization of France Télécom had been precisely that the funds raised could be invested in new technologies.[51] These funds were distributed among a vari-

Table 3-2. *Corporate Venture Capital Funds in France, 2000*

Fund name	Capital (millions of euros)	Targeted sector
Valeo Innovative Entrepreneur Fund	100	High-tech and e-business
Schneider Electric Ventures	50	New technology
Air Liquide Ventures	40	New information technology
Thompson-CSF Ventures	35	High-tech, electronics
PPR Ventures	25	Internet, e-commerce
ISCG (Shell France)	15	Petrochemical

Source: François Vidal, "De nombreux groupes industriels créent leurs propres fonds de capital-risque," *Les Echos*, April 6, 2000.

ety of goals, but the largest share, 91 million euros, went to a government-funded venture capital program called Public Funds for Venture Capital (Fonds public pour le capital risque, FPCR). This money was supplemented by 46 million euros in loans from the European Investment Bank (Banque Européene d'Investissement, BEI), which in June 1997, at the initiative of Strauss-Kahn himself, had taken on the role of supporting European venture capital funds. The combined 137 million euro fund was managed by France's state financial institution, the Caisse des Dépôts et Consignations (CDC). Within the CDC, a team of private and public experts allocated the funds among a broad group of private venture capital firms for investment.[52]

This new program, similar to the New Markets Venture Capital program of the U.S. Small Business Administration, had the goal of jump-starting the private venture capital market in France. Some FPCR funds supported experienced investment teams who needed help to raise new funds. But the CDC also targeted the FPCR at new venture capital teams, with the explicit goal of fostering new professional expertise in this area.[53] And in the short term, the effort appeared to be successful. The government had expected the program to induce matching investments from the private sector amounting to 600–700 million euros, and early trends in French venture capital suggested that it had met this goal. Indeed in 2000, Economics Minister Laurent Fabius created a second FPCR fund of 150 million euros, this one focused primarily on supporting biotechnology.[54] A third fund of this kind, created in February 2002, would focus on promoting later-stage investment.

Technology Transfer: A Continued Role for the State

The French government had long supported technology transfer through the Ministry of Research's Fund for Technological Research (Fonds de la recherche technologique, FRT). During the 1980s, technology incubation was typically funded entirely by the state and directed almost entirely at large enterprises.[55] In the late 1990s that changed. Henri Guillaume, France's minister of research, pushed for state funds to be shifted to encouraging technology transfer to small start-ups. One tool for this would be a new constellation of technology incubators funded jointly by industry and the government. Others included dedicated start-up funds, entrepreneurial competitions, and projects identified by France's new research networks (see chapter 2). The FRT budget attests to the shift in support from large to small firms in France (see table 3-3). Whereas only 6 percent of the FRT went to small enterprises in 1995, these received 51 percent in 2000. Conversely, large firms received 49 percent of these funds in 1995, but only 8 percent in 2000.[56] FRT funding also grew dramatically under Claude Allègre's tutelage, from 62 million euros in 1997 to 152 million euros in 2001.[57]

The new allocation in FRT funding supported the proliferation of high-tech incubators, or *pépinières*, across France. These incubators came in many varieties, but in general provided services and facilities, as well as finance, to new technology companies in their start-up phase. In December 2000 it was estimated that France had eighty such incubators, accounting for approximately 380 million euros invested in start-ups.[58] This number was diminutive, especially compared with the numbers in the United States (about 800) and Britain (about 200).

Half of France's incubators were privately sponsored. One-quarter (25 percent) were created by industry; another quarter (27 percent) were private French companies or branches of foreign incubators. By 2002, most of these private incubators had closed their doors.[59] Even though most did not survive, they nonetheless attested to the extraordinary enthusiasm for technology start-ups that swept France during this transitional period. They included Venture Park, started in December 2000 by Pixelpark, the Internet branch of Bertelsmann Publishing. It was run by a former McKinsey consultant, Fargha Moayed, and drew investments from Goldman Sachs,

Table 3-3. *Recipients of Funding from the Fonds de la Recherche Technologique (FRT), 1995–2000*

Percent

Recipients	1995	1997	1999	2000
Large companies	49	44	21	8
Small and medium-sized companies	6	26	37	51
Public organizations	21	26	37	35
Other	24	4	5	6

Source: Ministère de la recherche, "Le Projet de budget civil de recherche et développement BRD 2002," 2002 (www.recherche.gouv.fr/discours/2001/budget/bcrd.pdf).

DaimlerChrysler, and Deutsche Bank. Branches of Venture Park had already been opened in Berlin, Munich, and Madrid. They focused primarily on business-to-business Internet companies.[60] Other incubators in France were beachheads for foreign investors. Nasceno was Swiss-owned; Antfactory was a British group. Others were started by French companies. Chrysalead was the incubator for Danone; Bull created Bull Internet Incubator. Some were created by government laboratories. The Institut Pasteur, for example, created the Pasteur BioTrop incubator to support biotechnology start-ups.[61]

Many incubators that emerged in France were themselves new startups. One of France's early incubators, Tocamak, was cofounded by Jean-Luc Rivoire and Antoine Décitre in 1998. They took a minority stake in companies they promoted and in exchange offered those companies stock options in Tocamak.[62] Another incubator, Startup Avenue, collaborated with the Massachusetts Institute of Technology (MIT) to help large companies commercialize spin-off technologies as start-ups.[63] A third example, Republic Alley, was created in true start-up fashion: Faculty of Political Science (*Sciences Po*) graduate Laurence Edel and two friends renovated an old apartment building owned by Edel's grandmother near the Place de la République in Paris. They opened their doors in September 1999, with offices and advisory facilities to support ten new start-ups.[64] But most private incubators have not fared very well. Both Tocamak and Republic Alley, for example, moved out of incubation into pure venture financing.[65]

France's more successful incubators were created by universities or public research centers and jointly funded by industry. Between 1999 and 2002, for example, thirty-one public-private incubators were created through FRT support. They in turn backed 359 projects, leading to the formation of sixty-five companies.[66] Half of the funding for these incubators came from the FRT, amounting to 24 million euros per year for three years.[67] The remaining support came from private companies in their sectors. The long-term goal of these incubation projects was to create 800 sustainable new technology companies.[68]

In July 1997, Economics Minister Strauss-Kahn commissioned, in conjunction with Minister of National Education Claude Allègre and Secretary of State for Industry Christian Pierret, the report "Innovation and Technological Research." The so-called Guillaume Report—after Henri Guillaume, the former head of ANVAR who led the project—identified specific difficulties that France faced in promoting technologies in the new technology sectors. One problem was a lack of start-up capital, *capitale d'amorçage*. This was money that had to be invested even before a company was formed. Start-up capital is typically given to an individual with a promising idea or technology. It may finance an active patenting effort or make it possible for the research to move into the private sector.[69] To help rectify this problem, the government in 1999 set aside 15 million euros to create new *fonds d'amorçage*. The funds were administered by private investors, who applied to the government for access and who matched government support with their own sources of funding.

Some of these start-up funds, called thematic funds, were national in scope and focused on specific areas of innovation. I-source, created in May 1998 by the National Institute for Research in Computer Science and Control (Institut national de la recherche en informatique et en automatique, INRIA), specialized in information technology. Emertec in Grenoble, sponsored by France's Atomic Energy Commission (Commissariat à l'énergie atomique, CEA), focused on microelectronics and advanced materials. Bio-Am, located in Lyons, focused, as the name suggested, on biotechnology.[70] Two additional *fonds d'amorçages*, C-Sources and T-Sources, focused on multimedia and telecommunications, respectively.[71] Finally, regional start-up funds also emerged, cosponsored by local governments and industry with additional national support. By 2002, seven regional funds had been created.[72] Together national and regional start-up funds raised about 137 million euros from both state and private sources.[73]

Another popular way in which the government matched entrepreneurship with public funding was through a set of officially sponsored business contests. The largest of these was the "National Funding Competition for the Creation of Technically Innovative Companies," started by Claude Allègre in 1999 with 150 million euros in funding per year.[74] The competition proved so popular that the Ministry of Research doubled its funding in 2000, when it received 1,800 applicants and awarded 296 winners.[75] In 2001 the competition received 1,480 applicants and selected 238 winners. By September 2001, 500 new start-ups had been created as a result of the competition. Of these, 48 percent were in software and telecommunications, accounting for 54 percent of funds disbursed.[76]

Perhaps the most important role of the competition was to help private investors decide which start-ups to support. Contest entrants were evaluated by experts from ANVAR, first at the regional level and then at the national level. Roger-Gérard Schwartzenberg, the minister of research, also stressed the need to "accompany" competition winners through the development process.[77] Winners were incorporated into a network of entrepreneurs, and the government convened seminars to help the network members share information. And because ANVAR also certified companies for access to private venture capital, it was able to track the progress of the competition winners and help to coordinate other sources of funding for later stages of their projects.

The French Sénat, in collaboration with the business school ESSEC, created a similar competition, called "Tremplin Entreprise." This competition, instead of granting large financial awards, invited investors and corporate sponsors to participate in the process and to provide support to the winners. The temporary work agency Manpower, for example, offered an award to the project promising to create the most jobs. Arthur Andersen and Ernst & Young collaborated to provide coaching to contest winners. Microsoft offered technical support to winning software projects. And ANVAR declared all winning projects eligible for ANVAR aid. Most important, venture capitalists were invited to finance competition winners.[78] In 2000, the winners raised 18 million euros.

Conclusions

Given the break it represented with historical styles of innovation and social norms of risk and equality, why did France embrace private venture capital as a means of commercializing new technologies? In part, the effort reflected the success of U.S. venture capital institutions in funding technology start-ups during the 1980s and 1990s. But it also had its roots in restrictions imposed by the European Union, which limited government largesse. The French government's share of the national research budget had been steadily declining. Competition policy in the European Union had also limited the ability of the French government to support industrial innovation. Restrictions on state aid to industry have placed a limit on the scope of government generosity in competitive industries. And the liberalization of government acquisition policies required government contracts to be open to bidders throughout the European Union. Thus the European Union both limited government technology subsidies on the supply side and, by liberalizing acquisition policy, restricted supports on the demand side.

The irony of French venture capital was that greater private investment required greater government intervention. Far from reducing government programs for technology promotion, such programs actually increased during the period in which private equity financing grew. One survey found that 1,200 different kinds of aid were available to promote French start-ups at the European, national, and local levels in 2000.[79] Rather than espousing liberalization, the French administration saw itself as a kind of gatekeeper. It employed strong tax incentives to promote growth in private equity investment, but also controlled the direction and size of this investment. And it pursued these goals through an extraordinary variety of new institutions and regulations designed to forge a productive link between government-sponsored research and private investment. These institutional innovations included state-sponsored incubators, special start-up incentives for new firms, funds for investment in innovation, a new technology stock market, and a variety of tax incentives to encourage risky investment.

If the government played a strong role as market facilitator, it also paid close attention to the distributional implications of its policies. Powerful tax incentives encouraged greater private investment, in many cases from investors who might not otherwise have accepted the high risk inherent in funding technology start-ups. The French administration attempted to manage this risk by contributing state expertise to private investors. French private venture capital funds followed the guidance of a state agency, ANVAR. Government-sponsored entrepreneurial competitions helped to identify projects that represented promising technologies for commercialization. Government-funded incubators and start-up funds helped to identify and finance viable new companies. And while these measures may have looked overly interventionist from the American perspective, they appeared to work in the French context. After all, government agencies had always attracted France's most highly skilled graduates. These agencies had also been behind every major technological breakthrough in France in the postwar period. Successful venture capital funds rely on highly technical knowledge to make decisions, and in France much of this knowledge still resided within the state.

The government also strictly limited the amount that individuals could invest in venture capital at a favorable tax rate. In principle, this placed a ceiling on the risk that individual investors would take on, thereby limiting the distributional impact of risky investment. These measures also represented an effort to make private investment in technology start-ups compatible with the egalitarian preoccupations of French society. The problem was that the high risk of financing new technology start-ups also implied high rewards for success. But the French public was not necessarily ready to accept a newly wealthy class of successful technology investors. "We convinced the country to accept the idea of risk," recalled Stéphane Boujnah, an adviser to Dominique Strauss-Kahn, "but we failed to convince them of the need for a nouveau riche."[80] This commitment to egalitarianism may help to explain why the Jospin government accompanied new private investment opportunities with higher, rather than lower, taxes on individual wealth.

CHAPTER FOUR

Minitel and
the Internet

At first glance, one of the clearest signs of a poor fit between French economic institutions and the new information and communications technologies appeared to emerge in the realm of the Internet. By 2002, France lagged the United States and much of Europe in Internet penetration. Of course, the Internet *had* grown dramatically in France, from only 150,000 users in September 1996, to 1.3 million in January 1999, to 17 million in May of 2002.[1] But a comparison with its European partners nevertheless showed France to be a relative laggard. A survey conducted by the *Computer Industry Almanac* at the end of 2000 found that 15 percent of French adults used the Internet "on a regular or occasional basis," whereas 24 percent of Germans, 28 percent of the British, and 49 percent of Americans did so.[2] By mid-2002, 28 percent of the French used the Internet, compared with 39 percent of Germans, 57 percent of the British, and 60 percent of Americans.[3]

For many French observers of the new information and communications technologies, France's slow adoption of the Internet reflected a particular national deficiency. It became the focus of intensive domestic scrutiny of the country's distinctive statist heritage and what it implied for the adoption of a decentralized data network. "In the use of the Internet," wrote Guy Sorman for the French daily *Le Figaro*, "[we are] four times less connected than Americans or North Europeans. What are the reasons for this? They are first and foremost social. Stuck in a hierarchical vision of society, the administrative and academic elites feel that it is the task of secretaries, not 'Enarques' or 'agrégés,' to deal with text."[4] Charles Madeline, cofounder of the start-up incubator Republic Alley, echoed this concern: "Much of French culture is very centralized and administrative, which is the opposite to the [Inter]net. . . . This is a big barrier."[5] Paul-Andre Tavoillot, a reporter for *La Tribune*, suggested that "the new technologies completely confound the styles of decision-making of a centralized state."[6]

This cultural interpretation also permeated the French political debate about the Internet. René Trégouët, the French senator commissioned by Prime Minister Jospin to study France's Internet lag, expressed his view that "the Internet runs counter to a hierarchical society."[7] And Jacques Dondoux, French minister of commerce, agreed that "the 'French delay' is without doubt, first and foremost cultural." Thus for many, the decentralized, autonomous organization of the Internet appeared to conflict fundamentally with the traditionally centralized economic and social order in France.

But a closer look at the Internet experience in France suggests that this sort of cultural self-critique was largely misplaced. Instead, two closely related sets of problems impeded the emergence of the Internet. One problem derived from France's installed base. When the Internet first arrived in France, both customers and providers were accustomed to the technology, services, and business model associated with France's homegrown digital network, the Minitel. While not as flexible as the Internet, Minitel nonetheless filled valuable functions for many customers and service providers—through it one could procure financial services, order train and movie tickets, search business and residential listings, and send messages. This meant that the Internet in France had to be more useful than it was in other countries in order to persuade users to abandon Minitel. Like the inefficient QWERTY keyboard layout created in the nineteenth century that blocked more efficient key placements, Minitel locked users into a relatively inefficient technology that nonetheless still served an extremely valuable function.

A related problem derived from what the Austrian economist Joseph Schumpeter called "creative destruction." In his view, true innovation was nearly always destructive, because new products or procedures naturally threatened existing lines of business.[8] For most countries, the disruption that would be caused by the Internet was diffuse. Although it would claim some victims—Encyclopaedia Britannica, in a bid for survival, began giving its content away for free over the Internet in 1999—such companies were in no position to block the Internet as a whole. Instead, new companies emerged to pursue the new technologies, while existing companies formed new divisions in order to diversify their businesses. For most businesses, in other words, the new technology offered many potential advantages and few immediate disadvantages. It opened new areas of opportunity without challenging existing revenue centers.

In France, by contrast, the Internet emerged as a competing technology for companies already earning profits through Minitel. The national phone carrier, France Télécom, still enjoyed a stable income stream from Minitel. It therefore attempted to ease into the Internet in a manner that did not disrupt its existing or future business plan. France's sluggish response to the Internet was in this sense analogous to the slow adoption of high-definition television in the United States, where existing private companies resisted investing in a new technology for fear of cannibalizing their own lucrative businesses. The impediments that France faced in adopting the Internet were, in short, problems more familiar to the free market than to any centrally planned economy.

The Surprise of French Backwardness

National levels of Internet access are notoriously difficult to measure, and no standard methodology had yet emerged at the time of this study. But reputable polling organizations agreed that France was falling behind. Figure 4-1 presents a compilation of Internet use surveys conducted between 1997 and 2002. They combine survey sources and methods, and the results are not fully consistent. Yet taken together they present a coherent summary of national trends in Internet penetration.

The cross-country comparison presented in figure 4-1 reveals that France appears to have suffered from a dual lag. On the one hand, Sweden and the United States enjoyed an earlier Internet start than did France, Germany, or England. Thus part of the reason that France lagged in Internet

Figure 4-1. *Internet Users as a Percentage of the Population, 1997–2002*

Percent

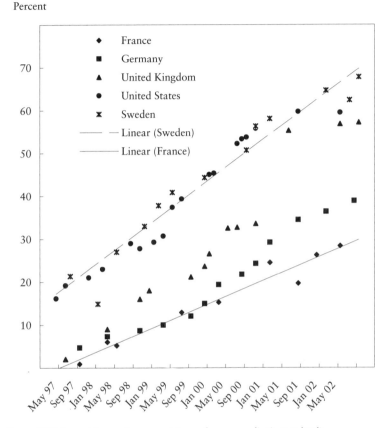

Source: NUA Internet Surveys (www.nua.ie/survey/howmanyonline/europe.html).

use during the late 1990s and early 2000s was simply that it came late to the Internet revolution. France in the fall of 2002 had an Internet penetration approximately equal to that of the United States in the fall of 1998.

Quite apart from France's late start, however, Internet penetration also grew more slowly there than in the United States or Sweden. In fact the Internet spread nearly half as fast in France as in the United States, measured by new Internet users as a percentage of the total country population. Internet penetration in both Sweden and the United States increased by approximately 10 percent of the total population per year between 1997 and 2002. In France, Internet penetration grew at just over 5 percent of the total population per year over the same period. If this pattern held, and given that approximately 30 percent of the French population had access to the Internet at the end of 2002, France could expect to reach U.S. and Swedish 2002 levels only by early 2008.[9] In other words, France's Internet lag was due only partly to the fact that it was slow to endorse the Internet. It also reflected the reality that French consumers were moving more slowly than others to embrace the new technology.

France also had fewer websites than other countries. Specifically, France had registered fewer hosts with the French domain .fr than had most other European countries. The OECD estimated that France in June of 2000 had one-and-a-half million web hosts, or about twenty-five per thousand inhabitants. This was fewer than Germany at the time, which had forty-five web hosts per thousand; fewer than Britain, with sixty-eight web hosts per thousand; and far fewer than the United States, with 280 web hosts per thousand inhabitants.[10] Yearly surveys of Internet hosts conducted by *Network Wizard* confirm that France continuously lagged behind its European counterparts in the number of websites available to Internet users (see figure 4-2).

Despite concerns about the compatibility of France's cultural heritage with the Internet, its slow move to the Internet was also surprising. First, France was the first country in the world to create a functioning national digital network. The Minitel system, a text-based network of terminals connected over the national telephone system, was installed beginning in 1982. Minitel development at the time was entirely state-funded, with terminals to access the service distributed at no charge. This early experience with Minitel trained the French population and business community in digital networks. By the time the Internet emerged in the early 1990s, French engineers were already highly skilled in digital technologies. When the World Wide Web Consortium sought a chairman in 1996, for example, it appointed the director of development at INRIA, Jean-François Ambramatic. Moreover, a community of nearly 25,000 profitable service providers had grown up around the Minitel, and these early French analogs to the American dot.com companies proved to be surprisingly profitable and agile. The Minitel experience also helped to accustom French consumers of all ages to seeking information and making financial transactions online. Thus for both service providers and digital service custom-

Figure 4-2. *Internet Hosts, 1995–2001*
Number of hosts per 1,000 population

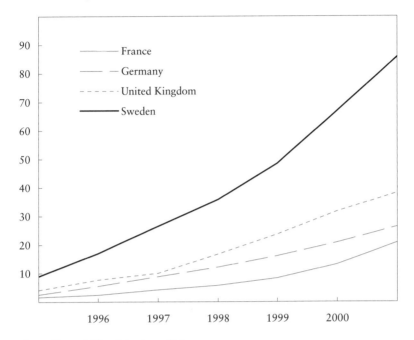

Source: Network Wizards (sss.isc.org/ds/).

ers, Minitel provided a training ground that should have prepared France for rapid adoption of the Internet.

Second, France had always been especially good at technically complex, networked infrastructure projects. This capacity had its roots in part in France's centralized and highly trained technical elite. France's government ministries were staffed with technicians and engineers trained in France's elite technical schools: the École Polytechnique, École des Mines, and École Nationale d'Administration (ENA).[11] Industry and the government shared expertise through a revolving-door system referred to informally as *pantoufflage*. This term, derived from the French word for a bedroom slipper, *pantouffle*, evoked the ease of passage from government to industry and back. For projects that required a high degree of coordination and technical know-how, the close ties between experts in industry and in France's government ministries permitted France to generate political support for complex technical endeavors, such as France's nationwide network of nuclear power generation stations (created under President Charles de Gaulle in the 1960s), and the Train à Grande Vitesse (TGV).[12] Not only was the TGV considerably faster than rival programs, including the Japanese bullet train Shinkansen and the German high-speed Inter City Express (ICE); it also appeared to be more economically attractive and had been chosen over the rival German system for inter-European routes, including the Thalys service from Paris to Brussels and Cologne, and the AVE service connecting France and Spain. France's network of technically skilled engineers played a particularly important political role. In the field of telecommunications, for example, they had provided an impetus to make France the first country in the world to move to fully digital telephone switching. "The ability of the *ingénieurs des télécommunications* to articulate a technological vision for French society in politically persuasive terms," explains Nicholas Ziegler, "reinforced their influence within the French state."[13] And despite radical changes in the organization of the French economy, France's technically trained elite and the system of *pantoufflage* still worked to create a strong link between industry and the government ministries at the end of the twentieth century. Their skills arguably should have made it possible for business and the government to coordinate their efforts in the creation of a successful Internet for France.

Government Support for the Internet

France's Internet lag was perhaps most surprising in light of pressure applied by the government to move France to adopt the Internet. In a speech given shortly after taking office in 1997, Prime Minister Jospin announced, "The ambition of my government is to facilitate the development of the information society in France while permitting as many people as possible to gain access to the new services." He warned that France's homegrown Minitel information network risked placing "a brake on the development of new and promising information technology applications." He therefore advised France Télécom to pursue a "progressive migration" from its Minitel network to the Internet.[14] Two months later, in a speech at the Communications Summer School in Hourtin in the Gironde, Jospin described France's entry into the information society as a "decisive challenge" for the future. As one commentator noted of Jospin's Hourtin speech: "The Internet is entering the political arena by the front door."[15]

As the Internet became a political topic, issues of fairness and equality of access were quickly thrust into the center of the French debate. Already in his 1997 Hourtin speech Jospin had cited the need to include everyone in the Internet revolution. President Chirac agreed, warning that a digital gap (*fossé numérique*) threatened to undermine state cohesiveness.[16] Subsequent surveys of French Internet use bore out these concerns. A survey conducted by Sofres for France Télécom in March 2002 found that 35 percent of French men, but only 23 percent of French women, were regular Internet users.[17] The Internet also accentuated the traditional divide between Paris and the provinces. The same poll found that 27 percent of Parisians regularly connected to the Internet, but only 12.5 percent did so in the rest of the country.[18]

From the beginning, therefore, France's Internet program included efforts to make the Internet accessible to the entire French population. One set of projects involved government programs to actively propagate the Internet. In 2000, the newly formed Government Action Program for the Information Society (Programme d'action gouvernemental pour la société de l'information, PAGSI) allocated 800 million euros to be spent over the next four years with the goal of extending Internet access throughout France. One flagship PAGSI program provided 250 million euros to equip and staff 2,500 "public numeric spaces," where 4,000 computer experts would be available to answer the general public's questions about the Internet.[19] Other PAGSI projects included the installation of 7,000 public Internet access points by 2003, funding to bring the Internet into French schools, and new information technology training programs.

Another prominent program focused on introducing Internet training into the French school curriculum. Because elementary and high school curricula in France are dictated from Paris, they are often at the forefront of new policy initiatives. Thus in 2000, Education Minister Jack Lang introduced a new Information and Internet Certificate (the *Brevet informatique et Internet*, or B2i). This required that students be tested in computer and Internet skills at the end of elementary (*école*) and middle school (*collège*).[20] An introduction to e-mail and the Internet, for example, would take place in ninth grade (*quatrième*). The new curriculum took effect with the beginning of school in the fall of 2002.[21] By 2002, however, much work still remained to equip the public schools to meet these requirements. In January 2000, French primary schools had one computer for every twenty-five students. In June 2001, only 35 percent of French schools had Internet access.[22] Another survey in August 2001 found one computer per six students in high school (*lycée*), one per fourteen students in middle school, and still only one per twenty-three students in elementary school.[23]

The effort to improve Internet access was not limited to pre-university education. In May 2000, Prime Minister Jospin announced the formation of a new *grande école* to be created at the Technopôle Château-Gombert, in Marseilles, that would focus on the Internet and offer a higher education degree in microelectronics.[24] And in 2001, Internet training was extended to adult education, with the creation of the new Information and Internet Certificate for Continuing Education (abbreviated as the unwieldy B2i FC-GRETA, or Brevet informatique et Internet, formation continue—groupement d'établissements).[25] This program emphasized technical training in computers and the Internet, as well as topics described as "information technology citizenship," including information privacy, intellectual property rights, and virus protection.[26] These new education programs suggested that the government was backing the Internet with more than just words.

A second set of government initiatives to promote the Internet targeted the high cost of Internet access. Studies by the OECD had shown a strong correlation between Internet access pricing in the advanced industrial countries and the growth of Internet penetration and e-commerce.[27] Concern in France focused on the cost of telephone service necessary to connect to any Internet service provider (ISP). In particular, the government pushed France Télécom to adopt an unmetered access pricing plan—a monthly rate allowing unlimited access to local phone service.

Access pricing quickly became the focus of a war of wills between new ISPs and the management of France Télécom, with the French government in the middle. In February 2001, leaders of France's largest Internet companies, including Jean-Marie Messier of Vivendi and Stéphane Treppoz of AOL France, published an open letter calling for France Télécom to provide universal flat-rate service to ISPs connecting to its service. Pointing out that only 19 percent of French households had Internet access at the time, in comparison with 29 percent in Germany, 35 percent in England, and 50 percent in the United States and Scandinavia, they called on the government to put pressure on France Télécom to implement a flat access rate. It was a step, they argued, that would be "key to the democratization of the Internet in France."[28]

Their message resonated strongly with the government. France's political leaders—President Chirac, Prime Minister Jospin, Economics Minister Laurent Fabius, and Industry Minister Christian Pierret—all endorsed a flat-rate service. Prime Minister Jospin, speaking at France's Fourth Fête de l'Internet in June 2001, reiterated the idea that a flat access rate would "democratize the Internet."[29] He noted that British Telecom and Deutsche Telekom had already begun offering such a service. Indeed the government promised that it would force France Télécom to provide a reasonable flat rate for the school year beginning in September 2001. France Télécom's oversight agency, the Autorité de régulation des télécoms (ART), began negotiations with ISPs and France Télécom to come to an agreement on a flat-rate service. In October 2001, a group of France's Internet service providers collected 190,000 signatures on a petition calling for affordable unlimited Internet access. Under pressure from the ART, France Télécom finally included a flat access fee in its rates catalog for 2002, one that lowered the cost of access for ISPs by an estimated 30 percent from 2001.[30]

The government was similarly interested in promoting affordable high-speed Internet connections in France. The Telecommunications Law of 1996, intended to liberalize access to local phone service, included restrictions pushed by France Télécom that blocked local communities from leasing high-volume data lines from private operators. The law also required that any telecommunications investment be amortized in at least eight years, raising the debt burden on local infrastructure projects to a prohibitive level for most communities. In Brittany, for example, France Télécom was able to negotiate with local communities to create a local high-speed optical network, called Megalis. The network was explicitly inaccessible to private companies, and it was expensive. Operating with a six-year contract that cost 60 million euros, the network provided thirty-three access points in local schools, the mayoral offices, and hospitals.[31]

In September of 2000, France opened France Télécom's "local loop" to competition. Because France lacked a dense network of cable television operators like that enjoyed in the United States, the government also supported the creation of alternative distribution channels. In July 2001, for example, France announced that it would make available 2.3 billion euros in government funds to make high-speed Internet access available in all parts of France. The government-run Caisse des depots et consignations would provide grants (300 million euros) and loans (2 billion euros) to local governments and banks to invest in high-speed communications projects. Proposed projects included ADSL alternatives such as fiber optic cables run on overhead poles alongside the electrical lines and local packet radio networks (*boucles locales radio*).[32]

All of these new systems were intended to compete directly with France Télécom's relatively expensive high-speed ADSL service, with the goal of eventually lowering high-speed access costs.[33] Consistent with this, in the summer of 2002 the government also called on France Télécom to lower the cost for ADSL access. The efforts proved relatively successful. By the end of 2002, the number of high-speed Internet users in France had grown to 1.7 million, up from 600 million only one year earlier. Interestingly, France Télécom argued that it could have lowered its ADSL rates even more, but was being forced by the government to keep them artificially high so that new competitors could stay in business.[34]

Minitel's Legacy

Given France's deep knowledge of digital networks, its proven capability in technically complex networked technologies, and strong government support, why did the Internet not emerge more rapidly? As suggested earlier, the core obstacle was the existence of a large installed base in the competing technology of Minitel. This information network, introduced in 1982, was known formally as Télétel. Based on the then new videotex technology, it emerged at the same time that videotex systems were being explored in Germany, Britain, and the United States. France was the only country to push the project to the broad public, a feat accomplished primarily by distributing free terminals to the majority of French households. Funded by the government and developed in government laboratories,

Minitel came to be an icon of the peculiarly French style of innovation in which the government picked technologies and pursued them in expensive and highly coordinated *grands projets*.

Minitel was from the outset a popular service in France. It provided easy access to information and services, including the phone directory, and in 2002 was used actively by an estimated 15 million people. In a 1999 survey, 22 percent of the French population reported using Minitel through private and public terminals.[35] By 2001, two-thirds of all houses and one-third of all businesses still had Minitel terminals. Indeed only in 1999 did the share of households with computers (30 percent in December 2000, up from 26 percent one year earlier) surpass the share of households with Minitel terminals (26 percent).[36]

Minitel was an especially popular forum for distance selling in France, or *vente par correspondence* (VPC). By 2001, some 50,000 transactions were conducted daily on Minitel,[37] including ticket reservations on the highly popular SNCF train system and purchases from major French catalog retailers like Les 3 Suisses and La Rédoute. In 1998, 10.4 percent of all consumer VPC in France occurred via Minitel.[38] Total Minitel sales in 1998, including train and theater tickets, were estimated at 2.3 billion euros.[39] By the beginning of 2001, Minitel represented approximately 18 percent of sales for the large catalog and distance sales companies.[40] For example, about 20 percent of sales for the retail catalog company La Rédoute occurred via Minitel.[41] Taking online services and VPC together, about 1.8 billion euros still passed through the Minitel system in 2001.[42] In comparison, Internet sales in France were relatively weak, though growing rapidly: from only 16 million euros in 1998 to 600 million euros in 2000.[43] Thus despite the rapid growth of the Internet in France, Minitel in 2001 still outsold the Internet in products and services by about four to one.

One secret of Minitel's success was its broad user base, secured by the decision of the French government to distribute the original Minitel terminal free to all French households. Like other big national projects in France that were substantially supported by the government—Airbus, the TGV— it remains unclear just how much it cost to set up the Minitel system, and therefore just how profitable it has been. Gérard Théry, head of France's Telecommunications Ministry when the Minitel teletex system was being developed and deployed, claimed that the initial cost of developing the Minitel network and distributing free terminals to French households was recovered by 1985. An external evaluation placed the break-even date substantially later, in 1998.[44] Whatever the case, Minitel reaped a generous annual revenue that continued to make it popular both with France Télécom and with the service providers that distributed their products via Minitel. As late as 1996, France Télécom was designing two new dedicated Minitel terminals, the Magis, which included a smart card reader to facilitate secure purchases, and the Sillage, essentially a phone with a small videotex screen.[45]

With the growth of the Internet, the number of Minitel terminals in use fell, but not precipitously. From about 6.5 million terminals in 1994, the number in use fell to 6 million in 2000, and to approximately 5 million in 2001.[46] But as of January 2001, 3.5 million computer users had also downloaded copies of Minitel emulation software.[47] Taken together, it appears that even in 2001 there were still more Minitel users than Internet users in France. The number of Internet users would not surpass Minitel users in number until sometime in mid-2002. Of course, estimates of Minitel and Internet use vary. France Télécom reported 15 million Minitel users in 2001, and approximately 11 million Internet users.[48] Another 2001 study found 18 million Minitel users and only about 7 million French Internet users.[49] Most accounts agreed, however, that despite the growing prevalence of home computers, Minitel still outranked the Internet in France in 2001.

Given the pervasiveness of Minitel, and the variety of proprietary services that it makes available, it may not be appropriate to compare French Internet penetration with that of its neighbors without also including Minitel penetration in the tally. The calculation must be made carefully, because many Minitel users also use the Internet. Taking care not to count dual users twice—France Télécom estimates that one-third of Internet users also use Minitel—the combined number of digital network users, including both Internet and Minitel, was a little over 22 million in France in early 2001. Thus about 37 percent of the population used some combination of the two.[50] This revised dual penetration rate still left France behind Sweden and the United States in digital network connectivity, but it did put France considerably ahead of Britain and Germany.

The presence of Minitel in France had contradictory effects on consumers' perception of the Internet. In what might be called the "Minitel effect," the French public was both more aware of and more accepting of the benefits of a digital network, especially regarding the potential for electronic business transactions, but also more hesistant to move to the Internet, since it already had access to a national network that offered many of the same features in a familiar format and with a high level of security. Thus while Minitel may have lowered French enthusiasm for the Internet, it nonetheless made them more comfortable than their European counterparts with the idea of electronic commerce. A Eurobarometer survey conducted in the fall of 1998, for example, found that 36 percent of the French population reported an interest in "obtaining information on, purchasing, or renting" products online, compared with 35 percent of the British and 30 percent of Germans. An even greater percentage, 42 percent of the French at the time, were interested in managing bank accounts or consulting the stock exchange online; only 30 percent of the British and 28 percent of Germans expressed such an interest. Finally, 58 percent of the French expressed an interest in accessing government information online, but only 45 percent of Germans and 40 percent of the British.[51] Yet this greater interest did not necessarily translate into greater Internet use. In the first half of 2000, a survey by the *Financial Times* found 2.37 million French citizens had connected to retail Internet sites, compared with 4.33 million German and 5.83 million British Internet users.[52] It appears that while Minitel had indeed introduced the French to electronic business models, it had also raised the threshold for giving up Minitel for the Internet.

France Télécom and the Internet

The emergence of the Internet came at a time of unprecedented economic liberalization in France. The Jospin government would eventually privatize more public companies than the six previous governments combined.[53] Shareholder value became a watchword among France's new business elite, and independent stockholders grew into a powerful class of investors.[54] Most significant for the Internet, France's public telecommunications provider, France Télécom, was partially privatized. After an initial stock flotation in 1997, and a second in 1999, the company had become 40 percent publicly traded. And nearly half of its traded stock was held by foreign investors, including the German telephone operator, Deutsche Telekom. Thus, although France Télécom was still majority state-owned, the high level of private ownership pushed the company to pursue a strategy of strong value creation. In principle, that should have created incentives to innovate that would drive France Télécom to embrace the Internet.

The route to privatization had been a long one. When the government of Edouard Balladur announced a plan to privatize France Télécom in August 1993, three-quarters of its employees went on strike, fearing that they would have to abandon the generous pay scale they enjoyed as public servants. Upon election in 1995, the new government of Alain Juppé again announced a proposal to privatize France Télécom. In response, 64 percent of salaried employees and 45 percent of white-collar workers at France Télécom went on strike. Michel Bon, a graduate of the Stanford Business School appointed by Juppé to run France Télécom, pushed aggressively for an issue of public stock in June 1996. In an intricate deal worked out with the employee unions, Bon arranged for employees to keep their status as public servants in exchange for accepting the flotation.[55] One of the reasons given for the sale of stock in France Télécom was that the money raised could be reinvested to promote new information and communications technologies.

On May 1996, in the midst of this difficult privatization process, France Télécom launched Wanadoo, an Internet service provider and French-language web portal that would become the most frequently accessed site in France.[56] France Télécom Interactive, a wholly owned subsidiary founded in January 1996, managed Wanadoo and another popular portal, Voila. Internet access services accounted for only 12 percent of Wanadoo's revenues.[57] In order to give it a good send-off, France Télécom had assigned to Wanadoo its highly profitable yellow pages (business directory) business. Wanadoo also participated in e-commerce, and acquired such popular French Internet retailers as Alapage, Marcopoly, and Librissimo. In 1999, Wanadoo made an initial public offering. The funds it raised helped it to compete in Europe's ISP consolidation process. In December 2000, for example, Wanadoo purchased the British Internet access provider Freeserve PLC for 2.4 billion euros. This made Wanadoo the largest Internet access provider in the UK and doubled the number of Wanadoo users to about 4 million. In December 2000, when Wanadoo acquired the Spanish phonebook publisher Indice Multimedia, business directory services still accounted for more than 80 percent of the group's revenue.[58]

Yet in comparison with similar services in other countries, Wanadoo's Internet performance was lackluster. Elie Cohen, a French political scientist and expert in industrial policy, accused France Télécom of a "lack of strong ambition" with respect to the Internet. He pointed out that Deutsche Telekom had made a far more successful move to the Internet. Its new ISP service T-Online had 1.8 million clients by 1998; at the same time, Wanadoo had only 100,000.[59] How had France Télécom fallen so quickly behind?

Of course, part of the problem was France's high connection fees. Whereas Britain and Germany had moved quickly to introduce a fee schedule that made possible a flat-rate Internet access fee, France Télécom had been dragging its feet. At the beginning of 2001, only Wanadoo was offering a monthly subscription that included the cost of the phone connection. Competing ISPs LibertySurf and Free.fr, which offered "free" Internet access, still required that members pay for local phone access. Some Wanadoo competitors did provide a flat-rate access to the Internet. Noos, for example, offered unlimited Internet access for 38 euros per month. AOL had also introduced unlimited access in France for 40 euros per month. Both did so by buying bulk access time that was charged by the minute and offering it as unlimited access to consumers. For AOL, however, customer access times proved greater than it had anticipated, and AOL was forced to raise its monthly flat rate to 65 euros.[60]

France's tariff structure may not have been ideal for potential Internet users, but the heart of the problem appears to have resided with Minitel. Although Michel Bon had initially been an outspoken advocate of the Internet in France, France Télécom hesitated to move aggressively away from Minitel to embrace the Internet. Instead, Bon adopted the language of fairness and equal access in justifying France Télécom's continuing support for Minitel. Speaking in Le Mans in 1998, Bon called for four measures that he argued would "democratize the Internet." Two of these measures would extend the services of Minitel: Internet messaging via Minitel; and access to the Internet over Minitel. Two other measures would provide wider access to the Internet itself: lower tariffs for access to Wanadoo, and special Internet offers to educational establishments. Bon's "democratic" approach, intended to resonate with political concerns about a digital divide, was in part an effort to shield consumers from the technical challenges of manipulating the Internet. "The complexity of the Internet," announced Bon, "must be hidden from the client."[61]

When France Télécom first launched Wanadoo, it had attempted to phase out Minitel, but quickly confronted two sources of opposition. First, companies that sold services or advertised over this network—the so-called "Minitel mafia"—feared switching to the Internet would deprive them of the income stream they earned over Minitel. Likewise, in 1997 France's own weather agency, Meteo France, had refused to provide its information free over the Internet while it was still making a profit over Minitel, so Parisian Internet users had to visit Yahoo! California to get a free Paris weather forecast. Reluctance by France's large Minitel information providers to move their content to the Internet resulted in an information vacuum that delayed the transition to the Internet for two or three years.[62]

Second, France Télécom itself came to recognize Minitel as a valuable source of revenue. Unlike the Internet, Minitel was conceived from the outset as a commercial network. It offered not only a secure billing and payment system, but, because users were charged by the minute for their connection to most Minitel services, it also offered a business model that had proved easy and profitable, not just for online retailing but also for information service providers. The key to the commercial success of Minitel services was its *kiosque* system for providing security and anonymity in billing. Under this system, France Télécom did not actually track what services individuals were using. Instead, different services were grouped into *kiosques* by the amount they charged per minute. *Kiosque* 3615, for example, provided public services starting at 0.37 centimes per minute; *kiosque* 3616 provided access to professional services, including the highly popular *Minitel rose* service permitting online romantic discussions. *Kiosque* 3605 included free services.

Unlike the Internet, where service providers looked to advertising as their primary revenue stream, the *kiosque* system of billing for services made Minitel a direct source of revenue for French service providers. Minitel also provided a low-cost centralized billing system. Connection fees were assessed through the telephone bill, and from these receipts France Télécom simply wrote a check to Minitel service providers. In 1996, the peak year

Figure 4-3.   *Services Sold over Minitel, 1988–2000*
Billions of francs

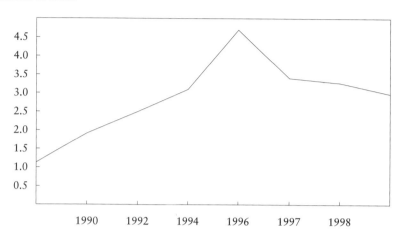

Source: Data compiled by author.

for Minitel use, France Télécom collected 7 billion francs and passed through 4.7 billion to the roughly 25,000 service companies.[63] Since 1996, Minitel revenues have been in steady decline (see figure 4-3). And because Minitel billed according to the number of access minutes, the decline in revenues reflected an underlying decline in customer access time. Time spent on Minitel fell 9 percent in 1999, 11.4 percent in 2000, and 23 percent in 2001.[64]

Despite the growing transition to the Internet, Minitel continued to be especially popular for certain segments of the population. Among those French 50 years and older, for example, 85 percent used Minitel.[65] Part of the appeal was the efficiency of accessing Minitel services. Whereas computers had to boot up, Minitel started immediately and connected rapidly. France Télécom claimed, for example, that making a train reservation was still more efficient over Minitel, requiring an average of 3.5 minutes, compared with 4.5 minutes on the SNCF Internet site.[66] One sign that Minitel still had advantages over the Internet was the fact that fully one-third of Internet users still also used Minitel to retrieve information in 2001.[67] Furthermore, because of its continued popularity, many service providers still relied heavily on Minitel. In 2001, an estimated 7,000 French service providers still offered their services exclusively via Minitel.[68] Even established international Internet brands like Yahoo! and Alta Vista, recognizing the continued enthusiasm for the proprietary network, began to make their services available via Minitel.[69]

Minitel had also been the training ground for many of France's successful Internet companies. Alapage.com, France's second largest Internet book distributor after Fnac, was created by Patrice Magnard as a Minitel service in 1988. Its web version was launched in 1996 and bought by France Télécom in October 1999.[70] Patrick Le Granche, founder of VID, an online software provider that offered versions of Word 3.0 that could be downloaded via Minitel, later moved to the Internet. His new company, Quarbon.com, had offices in Paris and San Jose and distributed free Internet tools and content.[71] Indeed, profits from Minitel gave many of France's Internet companies the capital to start their own Internet sites.[72] As one former government official noted in 2002, "Most of the firms making money on the Web today came from a Minitel background."[73]

Changing France Télécom

France's move to the Internet faced resistance among Minitel users and service providers, but it also faced challenges within France Télécom. The cause was partly financial. Even in early 2002, France Télécom was still earning more from Minitel than from its Internet services.[74] But the resistance to change also derived from the organizational ecology of France Télécom itself. Engineers within the management of the company, the so-called "*X-télécoms*" who had graduated from the prestigious École Polytechnique, had traditionally exercised strong control over technical decisionmaking within France Télécom. Thus even under a partially privatized France Télécom, this technical elite continued to speak out about the need to maintain Minitel. Jacques Dondoux, the *polytechnicien* responsible for launching Minitel in 1980, warned Jospin in 1997 that the French would not want to lose the security that the Minitel system provided. Dondoux had, after all, invented the very *kiosque* system that helped to make Minitel so secure.[75] Another *polytechnicien*, Olivier Bon, was running the Minitel and Internet Kiosque division (which included Wanadoo and other Internet sites) of France Télécom at the time. He reported that his goal was to slow the fall of Minitel in order to make a smooth transition to the Internet and mobile Internet.[76] Indeed the leadership of France Télécom was still dominated by *X-télécom* engineers with a soft spot for Minitel. Of the eleven members of the Executive Council of France Télécom in 2001, two had studied finance at ENA, and six others were *X-télécoms* from the École Polytechnique. Bon himself was an *Enarque* (a graduate of ENA).[77]

Others felt that Minitel was hindering a necessary move to the Internet, but making the transition proved difficult. Jean-Jacques Damlamian, the head of development at France Télécom, brought to the company a vision of what the Internet could mean for it. Beginning in 1998, he organized annual workshops called *journées de l'Internet Compagnie* at which France Télécom employees drawn from around France were introduced to the potential of the Internet. The first workshop, held for three days at La Défense in Paris, attracted nearly 3,000 employees, who were shown Internet applications that could make their jobs easier. To make the point, France Télécom began publicly advertising itself as the "Internet Company." In 2002, three years into the campaign, the company appeared to be turning around. But as Guy Carrèrre, head of research and development, warned, "We are not able to kill Minitel. It is too strong." He nonetheless projected that Minitel would be gone in two or three years.[78]

Torn between supporters and opponents, Minitel continued to play a role at France Télécom. The strategy was not to eliminate the project, but instead to leverage its success by forging deep links with the Internet. These links took a number of forms. On the one hand, a growing number of Internet users were using emulation programs that allowed them to access Minitel service from their desktop computers: 600,000 such programs were in use in 1996, 3 million in 2000. In October 2000, France Télécom introduced I-Minitel, a PC dial-in service offering high-speed access to Minitel. By March 2001, 500,000 people had downloaded the I-Minitel emulator and 200,000 were regular users. Consumers could also access Minitel directly over the Internet via Minitel's own Internet home page. And the French version of Windows 98 came bundled with software to access Minitel. In 2000, fully 82 percent of Wanadoo customers reported also using Minitel regularly, with many of them still returning to Minitel for particular services. Surprisingly, 14 percent of these customers started logging onto Minitel only after they had become Internet users.[79]

On the other hand, Minitel users were increasingly gaining access to Internet features. In 1998, France Télécom introduced the Minitelnet service, which provides the Internet-compatible e-mail account *le mel* to all Minitel users. A second initiative, initially called the Minitel-Internet and renamed the "screen phone," was intended to give Minitel customers direct access to the Internet as well. Its goal was not to compete with the Internet, but to provide simpler access for those who would not normally have it. Philippe-Etienne Zermizoglou, head of the screen phone division at France Télécom, noted in 1999 that "personal computer penetration will never reach 100 percent" and that there would always be "a large place for people who do not have a PC but who wish to access the Internet."[80] He described screen phones as a "guided" Internet experience and stressed that they were designed to "to make Internet access as simple as possible for the largest possible number of people."[81]

In October 1998, France Télécom joined with IBM to create an open standard software platform that would provide a common framework for screen phones to make them compatible with Minitel and the Internet.[82] The screen phone project of France Télécom and IBM was truly international—programmed in Java and using the international standard ISRF (Internet Screen Phone Reference Forum) developed by a global team of communications companies, equipment producers, and computer companies.[83] Billed as a means of "democratizing the Internet," the screen phone emerged as a compromise among the forces within France Télécom. As originally conceived, the screen phone was intended to be offered as a replacement to the traditional Minitel terminals that still found their place in most French homes.[84] In the summer of 1999, working screen phone models produced by Alcatel and Matra were tested on 500 volunteers in Toulouse and Paris. The Alcatel version was eventually selected and was later marketed under the name WebTouch. Alcatel pushed for France Télécom to give out the new WebTouch for free, as had been done with the original Minitel terminals. But given an estimated unit cost of 600 euros, the total price of this project would have come to several billion euros. France Télécom opted instead to sell the WebTouch phones.[85] In October 2000 it ran a 6 million euro marketing campaign to promote the new Minitel screen phone.[86] By March 2001, an estimated 100,000 of these devices had been sold.[87]

Conclusions

France lagged in its Internet use not because of excessive government regulation, but because of the excessive discretion of a dominant player with an economic interest in slowing the adoption of a new technology. The problem is familiar to all businesses that face rapid technological innovation. For most countries, the Internet represented an entirely new kind of business opportunity, without serious rivals. For France, by contrast, the Internet threatened to cannibalize the market of an existing technology: the highly popular and profitable Minitel system. It therefore faced opposition not only from Minitel's proprietor, France Télécom, but also from satisfied Minitel users and third-party service providers.

The irony of course is that Minitel was a state-sponsored project that was designed from the outset to be profitable. The Internet, in contrast, was a network for which commercial applications had been developed almost entirely by industry, and yet it proved to be surprisingly unprofitable for many of its service providers.

Minitel will probably always enjoy a mixed legacy. On the one hand, it created fertile ground in France for the Internet. When the Internet arrived in the late-1990s, French consumers were already highly knowledgeable about retrieving online information and conducting wireless online financial transactions. French businesses were already adept at providing online services. France's train company, the SNCF, was one of the first to sell tickets over Minitel; it also became the most popular commercial website in France. Customers of Cortal, a French brokerage, could trade securities over Minitel starting in 1993. When Cortal launched its Internet trading service (www.cortal.fr) in October 1999, two-thirds of its online traders shifted immediately to the Internet. One information-technology specialist reported that two-thirds of all Internet projects started in France ended up simply linking back to existing Minitel services.[88]

By 2002, French electronic service providers were gradually shifting from Minitel to the Internet. But they were doing so more slowly than their counterparts in other countries. But in comparison with Minitel, on which consumers and businesses spent about 1 billion dollars in 2000, the Internet was still the small brother.[89] A February 2001 Eurobarometer survey showed that only 21 percent of French Internet users shopped online,

compared with 35 percent in Germany and 37 percent in Britain.[90] Part of
the reason may stem from a disinclination to make purchases remotely. In
1998, the French spent 7.6 billion euros on goods purchased from electronic and paper catalogs, compared with 10.9 billion euros by the British
and 20.1 billion euros by Germans.[91] But the lag may also have been driven
by the continued popularity of Minitel as a site for electronic commerce.

There were also reasons to think that the Minitel technologies might yet
bear fruit in the multichannel world that would include third-generation
mobile telephony. France Télécom was trying, for example, to build on
one of the most popular aspects of Minitel, its security. It was therefore
planning to integrate into its homegrown short messaging standard (SMS)
a billing system called "kiosque SMS" that would draw on the kiosque
approach pioneered by Minitel. And it was collaborating with a Califor-
nia-based company, iPIN, to modify the Minitel payment system for use
on the Internet.[92] Whatever the fate of these Minitel spin-offs, it seemed
clear that France's slower adoption of the Internet had not been caused by
an overregulation of the economic sphere. Rather, the Internet grew slowly
in France primarily because it had to displace a useful, economical, and
profitable technology with an extremely broad base of users.

CHAPTER FIVE

Regulation and
the Internet

On May 22, 2000, Judge Jean-Jacques Gomez of a Paris appeals court called on the Internet portal Yahoo! to block French access to Nazi memorabilia sold on the auction site it runs. The decision responded to a lawsuit filed by three French antiracism associations, the International League against Racism (Ligue internationale contre le racisme et l'antisémitisme, LICRA), the French Union of Jewish Students (l'Union des étudiants juifs de France, UEJF), and the Movement against Racism and for Friendship among People (Mouvement contre le racisme et pour l'amitié entre les peoples, MRAP). Since 1972, antiracist groups in France had been empowered to bring lawsuits against provocation to racial hatred, and, under the popular 1990 *loi Gayssot*, the sale of Nazi memorabilia fell into that category.[1] Judge Gomez ruled that Yahoo! would be subjected to a 100,000 franc daily fine until it complied. One observer called the French decision "the modern-day equivalent of a border sentry."[2]

Critically, the Yahoo! case was not based on an objection to the principle of government regulation of Internet content. Yahoo! was already cooperating with the antiracism groups in France to block written pages that contained "negationist" content—assertions denying the existence of the Holocaust that are illegal under the *loi Gayssot*. And such domestic content restrictions were not limited to France. Yahoo! had been blocking commerce in other kinds of products that were illegal under U.S. law, including human organs, live animals, cigarettes, and child pornography.[3] Amazon.com, too, blocked the shipment of goods to countries where they were known to be illegal.[4] And at roughly the same time that the French Yahoo! case emerged, a Munich court opened an inquiry into the sale of copies of Hitler's *Mein Kampf*, banned in Germany, on Yahoo's German site. The case was later dropped, on March 21, 2001, when Yahoo! Deutschland was found not to have had full knowledge of these auctions, and because it had taken measures to block them.[5] Similarly, Japan and Britain had both investigated Yahoo! on the issue of pedophilia, the former for ostensibly having sold pedophile videos, the latter because pedophiles putatively use Yahoo! chat sites to contact their prey.[6]

What upset international observers about the French case, and formed the core of the Yahoo! legal defense, was the fact that the Yahoo! website in question was physically located in the United States and was not explicitly targeting French citizens. The French Yahoo! site, Yahoo.fr, which operated in the French language and denominated products in French francs at the time, was already blocking the auctioning of Nazi memorabilia. In contrast, the Nazi relics in question were being offered only in English, on a site based in the United States, and with prices given only in dollars.[7] Based on the French precedent, the fear was that pressure groups on any topic would be able to choose a jurisdiction in the world where that activity was banned, and then sue U.S. companies from there.[8] This precedent could lead to what one observer described as "a regime in which the most restrictive rules anywhere can be enforced everywhere."[9]

Yahoo! appealed the decision, arguing that it was not technically possible to entirely block access to such material by French citizens, and that even an imperfect filter would be expensive. The Paris court assembled a panel of three international Internet experts—American Vinton Cerf, British citizen Ben Laurie, and Frenchman François Wallon—to evaluate the possibility for a technical solution to permit Yahoo! to restrict French access to Nazi material. They estimated (in the absence of Ben Laurie, whose plane was grounded by heavy fog on his way to France) that about 70 percent of French users of Yahoo! could be detected via the identity of the server that they were using to connect to Yahoo! For the remaining 30 percent, Yahoo! would have to resort to other means, including voluntary nationality identification by users and a filter designed to identify French-language demands.[10] Taking all of the filter techniques together, the experts concluded that it would be possible to block approximately 90 percent of French users.

The non-French experts were critical of the filtering approach. Vinton Cerf later remarked that barring server access to French users was "at best a very weak mechanism." Ben Laurie called the filters recommended by the French court "half-assed and trivially avoidable."[11] Despite these criticisms, the court found on November 20, 2000, that Yahoo! was indeed capable of blocking illegal material from being accessed from France. The court pointed out that Yahoo! already employed technology that allowed it to identify French shoppers in order to post French-language advertisements.[12] And MSNBC had successfully employed geographically limited access to block U.S. viewers from streaming video coverage of the August 2000 summer Olympics.[13] Given the technical capacity to identify and block a large portion of French Internet users from accessing Nazi memorabilia on the Yahoo! auction site, the judge ruled that Yahoo! Inc. was "committing a crime on French territory, a crime whose nonintentional nature is evident but which is causing harm" to French antiracist plaintiffs.[14] In December 2000, Yahoo! asked a U.S. court in San Diego to block the enforcement of the French ruling in the United States.[15] It also nonetheless "voluntarily" banned the sale of all Nazi-related memorabilia on its site starting in January 2001.

Strangling the Internet?

The Yahoo! case was only the latest in a series of highly politicized incidents in which the emerging Internet had attracted unwelcome regulatory scrutiny by the French. Such cases caused foreign observers to worry that French regulation could strangle the Internet before it had a chance to grow. "If every jurisdiction in the world insisted on some form of filtering for its particular geographic territory, the web would stop functioning," warned Vinton Cerf.[16] That impression was reinforced by the rhetoric of French politicians, who regularly emphasized the threats that an unregulated Internet posed to France. President Jacques Chirac, speaking at a meeting of the Network Society in January 2001, warned, "the Internet today is putting our rights and our institutions to the test."[17] French econo-mist Jean Gadrey warned, "the Internet is high-tech neo-liberalism." Jacques Attali, adviser to the Jospin administration and chairman of a family of venture capital funds, worried that growing apprehensions con-cerning the Internet could lead France to shun it. Challenges he identified included "the weakening of borders, the globalization of sectors like edu-cation, health and justice, the preeminence of Anglo-Saxon law, which favors freedom of expression and the sanctity of contract, as opposed to Roman law, which gives weight to the protection of the individual against defamation."[18] Attali, himself an avid advocate of the Internet in France (he liked to use the metaphor of a seventh continent awaiting conquest), warned that such threats could lead the French government to overregulate.

Latent concerns about the Internet created a political opportunity for the Jospin administration. The challenge was to conduct a second phase of his policy focused on the "new economy," but without undertaking potentially expensive further economic reforms.[19] Beginning in 1999, the Jospin government therefore started pushing for a major legal package to regulate the Internet. The new Law on the Information Society, announced like his first initiative at the Communications University at Hourtin, would be ambitious in scope. It was to combine provisions protecting personal data, intellectual property, and consumer transactions, while at the same time restricting illegal content and adapting existing commercial regula-tions to the new medium. It would allow users to block all commercial e-mail; impose a "double-click" standard for the completion of an online contract; allow local municipalities to invest in high-speed networks; and ensure access to highly secure encryption. Its overall goal was to improve security in order to encourage broader use of the Internet. But the legisla-tive project, designed for political visibility, was ungainly and poorly con-ceived. By the time it was fully drafted, in 2001, many of its provisions were already outdated. Jean-Noël Tronc, Jospin's special adviser on the information society, suggested that the law be broken up and passed sepa-rately.[20] When Jospin lost his 2002 presidential election bid, Chirac's eco-nomics minister, Jean-Pierre Raffarin, nonetheless redrafted the legisla-tive package as the "Law for Confidence in the Numerical Economy."[21]

Behind the political rhetoric, however, France's approach to the Internet was surprisingly liberal. Most of the laws it put in place aided the Internet rather than restricting it. Tellingly, it opted not to create a powerful regulatory body to oversee the Internet. A survey conducted in July 2001 found that only 10 percent of French felt that the state intervened excessively in regulating the Internet, while 45 percent felt that the state did not intervene enough.[22]

The regulations France did enact were primarily intended to facilitate business transactions and reduce fraud over the Internet. In September 1998 a report of the Conseil d'Etat clarified that Internet sales would be treated as distance sales, giving consumers the right, among other things, to return purchased products within seven days.[23] In order to prevent fraud, the French Association for Internet Naming (Association Française pour le nommage Internet en coopération, AFNIC), created in 1997 to allocate the *.fr* domain, required registering companies to supply contact information and to have a physical presence in France. The law of March 13, 2000, changed the French civil code to give electronic signatures the force of law.[24] And a law of January 1999 gave French citizens access to encryption technology based on keys up to 128 bits in length.

The French encryption law was a particularly interesting case in which France adopted a far more liberal Internet policy than existed in the United States, where strong encryption technology such as PGP (Pretty Good Privacy) was at the time still restricted. Traditionally, France had limited publicly available encryption to a 40-bit key, a low level of protection that could be broken by a Pentium III computer.[25] This restriction was intended to allow government agencies access to private communications for law enforcement purposes. Then, in 1998, the French government received a report that a group of English-speaking countries—including Australia, Canada, Britain, New Zealand, and the United States—were collaborating on a data detection system, called Echelon, used to spy on international satellite communications. French officials suspected that this secretive system was targeting not just military but also government and commercial communications. After a year and a half of debate, in which France's secret service objected that it needed access to private communications in order to fight crime, the French Interministerial Committee on the Information Society (Comité interministériel pour la société de l'information, CISI) prevailed in legalizing strong encryption.[26]

The French government was actually wary of overregulating the Internet. This became clear in the interagency struggle to determine responsibility for regulatory oversight for the new network. Communications regulation in France had traditionally been divided between two agencies, one focusing on public broadcasts and the other on private communications. The Telecommunications Regulatory Authority (Autorité de régulation des télécoms, ART) regulated private communications. Created in June 1996, when the Senate voted to introduce competition in the telecommunications sector, the ART was an independent administrative authority charged with promoting competition and consumer protection, as well as mediating disputes between operators. Public broadcasts in France were regulated by a different agency, the High Council on Multimedia (Conseil supérieur de l'audiovisuel, CSA). The CSA had its roots in the period when audiovisual media, including radio and television, were controlled by the state.[27] Its claim to regulate the Internet derived from a third agency (the Comité supérieur de la télématique, or CST), created in 1993 to regulate the Minitel network, which was later placed under control of the CSA.[28] In this new arrangement, creators of Minitel sites were required to declare their content to the CSA.[29] The CSA maintained a monitoring office that surveyed traffic on Minitel, especially on the personal encounter sites called *Minitel rose*, in order to enforce standards of decency. In addition to monitoring Minitel content, the CSA served as an arbitrator in disputes among audiovisual providers.

The Internet confounded the division of labor between the CSA and the ART. On the one hand, because of its history of regulating Minitel, the CSA seemed like a likely candidate for regulating the Internet. Some of the CSA's mandates for radio and television, such as the protection of young audiences, might logically have justified extending its scope of competency to the Internet. On the other hand, the personal nature of much Internet content suggested that it was more akin to telephone communications. Indeed a report commissioned by the prime minister on the subject of Internet regulation recommended that the CSA not be given control over the Internet, precisely because it might prove overly restrictive.[30] The draft Law on the Information Society adopted this recommendation, granting predominant control of the Internet to the ART. The CSA would retain an oversight role, but only in audiovisual content provided online.[31]

And tellingly, neither agency would have discretion over enforcement, a responsibility that was explicitly left to the French courts.[32]

In June 2000, France also created an entirely new administrative authority to deal with regulatory issues that the Internet had raised, including such novelties as Internet auctions and the regulation of search engines. Called the Forum on Internet Law (Forum des droits d'Internet), it brought together representatives of private, public, and consumer interests to discuss emergent issues in Internet content and security. The French referred to this approach somewhat misleadingly as "coregulation." The forum had a budget of 10 million francs and offered its nonbinding recommendations to the public authorities.[33] Its discussions embodied France's dual efforts to consider and to monitor legal issues related to the Internet, but not to overly tax the new medium. "This elaborate forum for discussion . . . among often opposing interests," wrote Christian Paul, "will offer for all an effective method to illuminate an evolving society."

Regulating Content

French regulatory treatment of the Internet underwent considerable change between 1996 and 2002. Initially court decisions were marked by diverse interpretation. In March 1996, the Jewish student organization UEJF charged nine Internet service providers (ISPs), including Compuserve, with supporting sites with revisionist perspectives on the Holocaust. Judge Jean-Pierre Marcus of the Tribunal de grande instance de Paris recognized the grievance, but found that it was technically impossible for ISPs to filter the sites they hosted.[34] Two months later, in May 1996, Sebastian Socchard, head of Worldnet, and Rafi Haladjian, head of Francenet, were both charged with and convicted of distributing child pornography because their services hosted sites that did so.[35] In response to the apparent lack of uniformity, Telecommunications Minister François Fillon introduced an amendment to the 1986 telecommunications liberalization law that placed a high burden on Internet service providers to survey the content they provided. This approach was not unprecedented. It extended to the Internet jurisprudence that had already been applied to Minitel, in which service providers were conceived legally as editors and therefore held strictly responsible for the legality of the information they disseminated. It also paralleled legislation in the United States, where Congress limited Internet content with the 1996 Communications Decency Act.[36]

At stake was the level of responsibility to which Internet service providers and Internet portals should be held for content provided on their sites. The answer depended in part on what one thought the Internet was. Should ISPs and web portals be treated as analogous to newspaper editors, who oversee content, or to newsstand proprietors, who simply distribute existing publications? As editors, they would be held responsible for the content of web pages available at their sites. As newsstand proprietors, they could be assumed to know little or nothing of the content of the material to which they provided access. The problem was that early legislative efforts in France, as in the United States, tended toward the editorial analogy. This approach placed a high burden of responsibility on ISPs and portals for the content accessible through their services. It responded to the apparent lack of legal redress for plaintiffs injured by Internet sites.

One victim of the new legislation, Valentin Lacambre, operated the free website hosting facility Altern.org. In 1998, acting on the Fillon amendment, a court of appeals in Paris forced Lacambre to pay 400,000 francs in restitution to supermodel Estelle Hallyday for hosting a personal website that showed her naked. At the time, Altern.org hosted 47,634 personal websites. Lacambre settled the Hallyday suit (he paid 70,000 francs), but was then sued again for 2.5 million francs for hosting a website that was found to infringe on the trademarked words of the fictional cartoon character Calimero. Critics at the time noted that Calimero's exclamation— "C'est trop injuste!" (It's just not fair!)—seemed to capture Lacambre's own situation precisely.[37]

Following a public outcry over the fate of Lacambre and his company, AlternB, Socialist deputy Patrick Bloche proposed new amendments to France's 1986 Freedom of Information Law. These amendments, adopted June 28, 2000, removed liability from web hosts and ISPs for content on pages they hosted. But they left two exceptions. One, private sites were required to register with hosts, and hosts had to investigate if they were contacted by a third party alleging that web content hosted on their service was illegal. Two, ISPs were required to offer filtering services to their clients.[38] In decisions of December 8, 1999, and January 31, 2000, the Tribunal de Nanterre affirmed that site managers had to "take the necessary precautions to avoid hurting the rights of third parties."[39] Both the majority and the opposition supported the Amendment Bloche, which had been introduced by Alain Madelin (Démocratie libérale, DL) with backing from the Gaullist RPR (Rassemblement pour la République) in March 2000.[40]

The requirement that private site holders register their identity (name and address) with hosts was hotly attacked by Internet organizations in France, with outside support from the American Civil Liberties Union and the Electronic Freedom Foundation, as well as from France's own Communist Party.[41] Even Lacambre, the former head of AlternB, precisely the organization that the Bloche amendments were designed to protect, shut down his server in protest the day after the amendments were put in place, putting approximately 48,000 sites out of business. Lacambre recommended that the sites he had hosted consider instead seeking hosting on anonymous foreign servers.[42] Catherine Tasca, minister of culture and communications, nonetheless justified the new standard, noting, "Being a site manager [*hebergeur*] does not make one less of a citizen, and certain content cannot be left freely accessible."[43]

French Language and the Internet

Language proved a challenging regulatory area for France. In October 1996, two French language associations had brought a case against Georgia Tech Loraine, the French campus of the Georgia Institute of Technology, a U.S. university, on the grounds that it provided only English-language content on its French website.[44] Specifically, the school had run afoul of France's *loi Toubon* of August 4, 1994 (law 94-665), named for France's former minister of culture and *francophonie* Jacques Toubon and which enforced the use of French in commercial speech. Under the law, accredited associations could sue to defend the French language. Georgia Tech Loraine denied doing anything wrong, claiming that its French website was part of its American campus. The case was eventually thrown out because of procedural problems (the language associations had neglected to notify the prosecutor before filing the lawsuit, as was required by law). But Georgia Tech nonetheless began providing content in French as well as German.[45] The case made language an axis of cultural concern about the rise of the Internet in France. It also seemed to reflect a broader cultural unease about the role of the French language in the context of globalization.

The legal requirement to use the French language had not been created specifically for the Internet. Legislation imposing the use of the French language had a deep history in France. The use of French was first required by a 1510 ordinance of Louis XII, amplified by the 1539 ordinances of Viller-Cotterets, and more recently addressed under the Law of 2 Thermidor of the French Revolution. The modern standard for the use of the French language was established in 1975, when legislation made French mandatory for all written and spoken transactions, as well as in work contracts, bills, product instruction sheets, and product guarantees.[46] Among the victims of this early legislation were the Paris Opera, for printing a handbill in English, and a French cigarette manufacturer that advertised its product as sporting a "new filter."[47] The increased flow of intellectual and real goods across national borders only intensified administrative concern over the use of the French language. Recent lawbreakers targeted by the loi Toubon included *La Poste*, for naming its express service "SkyPak," and the Walt Disney Company, for the English-only labeling on some of the products sold at its store on the Champs Elysées.[48] It was a sign of the heightened concern that globalization posed a real threat to the French language that on June 25, 1992, an amendment to the constitution of the 5th Republic officially declared: "The language of the Republic is French."[49]

In fact, the Internet did pose special problems for the use of French. First, almost all of the technical terms related to Internet functions were of English origin. In March 1999, and again in May 2000, the Ministry of Culture's General Commission on Terminology and Neology proposed new French terms that would be the equivalent of currently used English words related to the Internet, including alternatives to hacker (*fouineur*), spamming (*arrosage*), and even the World Wide Web itself (*toile d'araignée mondiale*, or TAM).[50] This creation of often humorous new terms to adapt the French language to changing technology was not only or primarily focused on the Internet. Advances in other fields such as automobiles, nuclear engineering, and even the new European currency had evoked creative French neologisms. But in the case of the Internet the new alternatives had largely failed to enter common use.

Second, the Internet raised the question of the rights of all countries to have their own languages used within their borders. The 1994 loi Toubon in fact broadened the existing standard for the use of French, shifting from a French-only standard to emphasizing instead the need for multilingual Internet content. By this new standard, French was required to be "at least as prominent as other languages in commercial areas." This embrace of *multilingualisme* was in part a recognition of the increasingly globalized world that the Internet had helped to craft. But it also represented a growing awareness of linguistic and cultural diversity. Catherine Trautman, minister of culture and communications in the Jospin government, defended the loi Toubon thus: "To express oneself in one's own language is a cultural act. We must put French on the web. The lingua franca of the web is not English; it is computer code. . . . We must not favor 'monolingualism' in one direction or another. We must fight the battle now."[51]

The impact of the Internet on the French language was not entirely negative.[52] Francophone countries, including France, had seized on the Internet as a tool for bringing the world's French-speaking patchwork closer together. French-speaking states represent 500 million people in the world, one-twelfth of the world population. They represent a combined gross domestic product (GDP) of 2 trillion euros, roughly one-tenth of the world's total production. Although numerous, these countries were also geographically and economically fragmented. They represented 17 percent of world trade, for example, but only 14 percent of that trade was among themselves.[53] The Internet had the potential to overcome the barriers of distance that separated France from its former colonies. This was the message delivered to the Seventh International Francophone Summit held on November 16, 1997, in Hanoi, Vietnam.[54]

The idea of a francophone Internet struck a chord among many French-speaking nations and proceeded quietly but assuredly. At a planning meeting on May 21, 1997, in Montreal, delegations representing thirty-five francophone countries adopted a plan to develop a francophone Internet. France had offered to pay a third of the budget, or about 2 million euros yearly—a small sum beside the nearly 200 million euros that France dedicated annually to promoting the French language at home.[55] The resulting project, the Fonds francophone des inforoutes, was launched in the summer of 1998. By September 1999, one year later, it had already received 530 project proposals and funded sixty-three projects, including special French-language websites, electronic catalogs, and e-mail networks, with grants totaling about 30 million francs. The process was designed from the outset to be inclusive. All proposals had to be submitted jointly by at least three member states and include at least one developing country. And the projects were bearing useful fruit. One successful effort was the Virtual Francophone University, headed by Didier Oillo, which used distance-learning technology developed by the National Telecommunications Institute in Evry to provide content from French universities to their counterparts in Dakar, Senegal, and Yaounde, Cameroon.[56]

Providing public funds to give France a greater place on the Internet was also a domestic priority. On top of the 2 million euros that France made available for the project on *francophonie*, it provided an additional 2 million euros to put some 50,000 French literary works online, and 2.4 million euros for digitizing France's "artistic patrimony."[57]

Despite their likely real impact on French-language content on the web, these projects showed limited success in shifting the overall penetration of French-language sites on the Internet. One study found that 6 percent of Internet servers in May 1997 used the French language.[58] Subsequent studies in 1999 found that only 1.5 percent of Internet sites were in French, compared with 97 percent in English.[59] In 2002 a third study found that 3 percent of total Internet content was in French, 75 percent in English.[60] Yet even with the limited (if growing) French content, French Internet commerce sites would enjoy a potential advantage. The worldwide francophone market was estimated at about 160 million, not a small consumer base by any standard.[61]

The European Union and the Internet

The cross-border nature of Internet crime led many European leaders to conclude that the new digital network should be regulated at the international level. Martin Bangemann, European Union (EU) commissioner on telecommunications and industrial affairs, warned that in the absence of international regulatory agreement, Europe and the United States were likely to mire the Internet in conflicting national regulations.[62] French experts and politicians had long supported a European initiative to tackle Internet crimes. In 1995, Hervé Bourges, the head of France's own multimedia regulatory agency, the CSA, called for an international law governing the Internet, a "universal legal framework scaled to the global scope of the Internet," and proposed that his own organization be mirrored by a new regulatory agency at the European level.[63] President Chirac also embraced this idea, arguing that the Yahoo! case "emphasizes the emergence of an ethics for the network society, which, beyond existing holes in the law, imposes a common law for the Internet."[64] He pushed in particular for cooperation and a common set of European standards on "cybercrime." The Lisbon Summit of the European Union, convened in March 2000, seemed to provide a mandate for EU regulation. It highlighted cybercrime as a specific area in which the EU should act, and set a deadline of 2002 for harmonizing member-state regulation of the Internet.

Given this emphasis, one surprise was that the European Union itself did not play a larger role in Internet regulation. In principle, the EU should have had little problem taking on the task. A European Internet would have reinforced the common market goals laid out in the Single Europe Act. A single set of rules governing the Internet in Europe would have sent a powerful signal about the future of the European common market. Moreover, the timing for EU regulation was just right. The Treaty on the European Union entered into force in 1993, the same year that the Mosaic Internet browser, developed in Europe at the Organisation Européene pour la recherche nucléaire (CERN), introduced nontechnical computer users to the Internet. But the European Union was slow to respond, waiting seven years to reach agreement on Internet regulation. The Lisbon summit proposed to provide a common basis for Internet commerce so as to increase Internet access, lower costs, provide greater security, and make Europe the most competitive and dynamic region in the world by 2010. But by the time the EU administration in Brussels had acted, member states were well advanced in working out their own regulatory strategies. Already playing catch-up, the European Union tried and failed to wrest Internet regulatory issues from the control of its member states.

One early battle emerged over the standard of consumer protections that Internet sales should receive. In 2001 the European Commission adopted the Rome II green paper proposing that e-commerce distributors be required to meet the noncontractual obligations—including product liability and defamation standards—of the country in which their goods were sold. This country-of-destination principle had been intended to promote consumer confidence in e-commerce. Lionelo Gabrici, a spokesman for the European Commission, stated that "a lack of consumer confidence is the main thing holding up the development of e-commerce in Europe."[65] But the new proposal immediately faced opposition from Europe's Internet providers and publishers, as well as from Antonio Vittorino, European commissioner for justice and home affairs, and from members of the European Parliament.[66] Eventually the EU returned to a conventional country-of-origin standard.

Another characteristic case of EU regulatory treatment concerned unsolicited bulk e-mail, or spam. The European Commission appeared to be worried that excessive spam would discourage potential new Internet users. Estimates of the price of spam to e-mail users, measured as the extra connection time necessary to download unsolicited e-mail, came in at about 30 euros per Internet user per year.[67] Worldwide, the cost of spam was estimated at 10 billion euros annually. But if the costs to consumers were high, the costs to the direct mail industry of restricting spam were also potentially high. By introducing consumers to attractive new products, direct marketers claimed to increase the quality of the consumer experience. These claims notwithstanding, spam was perceived in Europe as a problem with primarily American roots. A study commissioned by the European Union found that 80 percent of spam in Europe originated from U.S. sites such as Amazon and Travelocity.[68]

Two responses were proposed. The "opt-in" model required that consumers have "explicit choice" about whether information they submitted over the Internet could become part of commercial mass mailing lists. In other words, they would need to indicate actively that they wished to receive e-mail. Supporters of the opt-in model argued that it would increase consumer confidence and lead to greater economic use of the Internet. The alternative "opt-out" model required that companies permit consumers to request that information they submitted not be used in bulk e-mail lists. Ireland, the UK, and Luxembourg supported the opt-out system. The remaining European countries supported the opt-in system. Oddly, French legislators had already adopted the opt-out standard, even though the

French government formally supported the opt-in standard for a new European directive.

A third solution embraced by many European countries was to provide for a privately managed set of suppression lists. Such lists would contain the names of individuals who wished to remove their names from e-mail solicitation lists. National legislation in France already required that any distribution list first be matched against a suppression list in order to ensure that members of the list were deleted. Countries with such private initiatives to pursue suppression lists included Germany, Sweden, Netherlands, Finland, UK, Norway, Spain, and Italy.[69] France also included provisions for a national suppression list system in its draft Law on the Information Society, and France's association of direct market retailers, Fédération des entreprises de vente à distance (FEVAD), sponsored its own list at www.e-robinson.com.

Past EU directives had been ambiguous about the treatment of unsolicited e-mail. The European Telecommunications Directive of December 15, 1997,[70] did not specifically address e-mail, leaving member states to their own discretion in deciding whether to pursue the opt-in or opt-out strategy.[71] In transposing this directive into state law, five EU countries explicitly chose the opt-in approach: Germany, Denmark, Finland, Italy, and Austria.[72] In contrast, the European E-Commerce Directive of June 8, 2000,[73] specifically promoted the opt-out provision. This standard was favored by almost every direct marketing organization in Europe, including the Internet Advertising Bureau and the International Chamber of Commerce. The directive required direct marketers to incorporate an option for site users to opt out. It also provided for privately held suppression lists and required direct marketers to filter their mass mailings using these lists.[74] Additionally complicating the issue, the European Union had adopted a strict law on data privacy. The data protection provision in a directive from October 1996 set standards of "unambiguous consent" and "fairness of processing" for the collection and use of consumer data.[75] The French association that oversees data protection, the National Commission on Computing and Freedom (Commission nationale de l'informatique et des libertés, CNIL), argued that mass electronic mailings, because they required the collecting of e-mail addresses, must be governed by this 1996 data protection directive. CNIL claimed that the opt-out principle of the e-commerce directive ignored the principles of the data protection directive, especially the requirement of fairness of processing.[76] The European Union, for its part, was loath to extend existing data protection standards to Internet applications because of the likely impediment doing so would pose for the liberalization of financial services. It could particularly hurt the exchange of credit, financial, and insurance information. A study by Ernst & Young, for example, found that a transposition of the EU regulations on data protection to the United States would lead to a loss of 16 billion dollars in financial services and an additional 305 million hours spent on personal finances.[77] Robert Litan of the Brookings Institution warned that it also risked raising barriers to new and often innovative firms that sought to market new financial products.[78]

In a September 2001 vote, the European Parliament struck down the opt-in model by a wide margin (204 to 129, with 155 abstentions).[79] On December 6, 2001, the Council of Ministers of the European Union chose, despite the parliament's opposition, to favor the opt-in approach to restricting commercial e-mail.[80] Finally, in May 2002, the European Parliament approved an anti-spam provision embracing the opt-in standard. The directive was endorsed by the European Council in June, but would take three years to be transcribed into country law.[81] And by that time national approaches would likely already be firmly established. Although France had already incorporated the opt-out standard into its draft Law on the Information Society, how the new European directive would be transcribed into French law remained unclear in 2003.

Conclusion

The surprise about France is not that it worked to regulate the Internet, but that it did so gradually, and with close attention to the likely impact of its rules on the growth of the new medium. "In the broadest political sense," writes Harvard Business School professor Deborah Spar in *Ruling the Waves*, "the most remarkable thing about cyberspace may be just how unremarkable it actually is. For there will be rules in cyberspace, and governments will help to craft and enforce them."[82] It is a view shared by Lawrence Lessig, a Stanford University law professor and visionary of Internet law: "As the Net changes to enable commerce, one byproduct of this change will be to enable regulation."[83] Internet commerce itself created the incentives to seek regulation as a means of lowering the costs—including security, authentication, and certification—of doing business online. Most French laws that addressed the Internet directly were intended to create a more secure environment for Internet transactions, and they were greeted with support.

The challenges France faced emerged in the context of older laws designed for a world with clearer borders. Cases involving anti-Semitism and Nazi memorabilia continued to challenge court interpretation. The Yahoo! case, for example, emerged again in 2002. Disappointed with the outcome of their suit against the company, the original plaintiffs filed a new complaint in October 2001 against Timothy Koogle, the former CEO of Yahoo! Koogle was personally charged with inciting racial hatred, a criminal charge with a maximum sentence of five years in jail. In May 2002 a Paris criminal court found itself competent to hear the case.[84] Koogle was acquitted of the charge in February 2003. Meanwhile other cases had emerged that emphasized just how difficult France's challenge would be in targeting anti-Semitic material on the Internet. In particular, what role should French Internet access providers play in this protection?

The difficulties they faced had been highlighted by a new set of legal issues raised by the anti-Semitic website, Front 14 (www.front14.com). Hosted in Alaska by General Communications, the site included, but was not limited to, racist and anti-Semitic material. The case also arrived in the court of Jean-Jacques Gomez, when the antiracial hatred organization J'accuse! brought suit against France's association of web access providers, the Association des fournisseurs d'accès et de services Internet (AFA). J'accuse! asked the judge to force thirteen French ISPs, including France Télécom and AOL France, to block access to Front 14.[85] In a July 2001 decision, the French judge refused to do so. Gomez noted two problems that would continue to plague France's efforts to regulate Internet content. First, Front 14 also hosted sites that were not illegal by French law, and banning those would constitute a breach of free speech even by French standards. Second, AFA argued that ISPs should not be forced to become the Internet's police.[86] In this case Gomez's view appeared to have softened somewhat, and he concluded by "inviting" access providers to filter out Front 14, but not forcing them to do so.

CHAPTER SIX

Silicon and
the State

New technologies have historically helped to reinforce, rather than undermine, the authority of the nation-state. Telegraph and rail drew nations together as a polity. Industrial production increased wealth and with it government revenues. New weapons technologies helped to build nationalism and win wars. Innovations in energy and agriculture made nations more self-sufficient. Yet the new information and communications technologies emerging today appear to run counter to this trend. Rather than reinforcing boundaries, they seem to transgress them. Rather than bolstering the state, they appear to undermine it. This research into French innovation policy began with an apparent challenge: could France promote new technologies and achieve economic growth without undermining the historic role of the state?

The success of the United States in the new information and communications technologies created an expectation that liberal market institutions defined the best and perhaps only environment in which these new technologies would prosper. Observers concluded that success in the Internet economy demanded a model of business-government relations that was deregulated and decentralized.[1] Researchers in industrial innovation pointed specifically to the role that liberal labor policies, liberal capital markets, and liberal corporate governance regimes played in promoting radical new product innovation. The implication was that countries embracing these liberal market features would enjoy a comparative institutional advantage in the new technology sectors and would outperform their neighbors.[2] Thus as the new information and communications sectors came increasingly to dominate economic production, countries with corporatist or statist economic regimes would feel pressure to adopt liberal institutions. The result was thought to be a convergence on an institutional best practice that would require many countries to fundamentally rewrite their market rules.

The French case offers some preliminary evidence that the new technologies of the third industrial revolution may continue to be compatible with, and will perhaps in the long run enhance, state activism. It suggests, first, that governments with the proper capacities can still play a role in picking technology winners. Although the Jospin government moved to promote private sources of investment in new technology ventures, it did not seem to believe that individuals alone should make critical decisions about capital allocation. What emerged instead was a novel set of institutions to marry private capital with public guidance in investing. The government funded a group of technology incubators focused on start-ups in technology sectors that it believed would offer the greatest prospects for commercial success. It established a new set of funds for investment in innovation (Fonds communs de placement dans l'innovation, FCPI) that offered attractive tax incentives for private venture capital, but only if they focused on start-ups that had been certified by the state agency ANVAR (Agence nationale pour la valorisation de la recherche). And publicly sponsored entrepreneurship competitions helped to guide venture funding to new companies deemed to be promising by judges from government agencies. This directed approach to investment may even have made sense in the French context, where the French state still employed many of France's most talented researchers and engineers, and a new venture capital community had relatively limited experience in choosing winning technologies.

Second, the French experience suggests that high-tech entrepreneurship can be made compatible with demands for economic fairness. France's stock-option regime, for example, encouraged stock-option compensation for those willing to underwrite risky ventures. But it also taxed capital gains at a high rate to discourage companies' use of stock options as executive compensation. This approach, while fiscally complex, nonetheless helped to combine a culture of genuine risk-taking with restraint on executive pay. France also sought to limit the distributional impact of risky, and potentially very profitable, early-stage investments by placing a 75,000 franc yearly cap on the amount that individuals could invest in these funds and still receive a favorable tax rate. This strategy may ultimately prove inefficient—it is after all the wealthiest investors who are best placed to absorb the risk of technology investments—but it did respond to political concerns about the distributional impact of private technology.

Finally, France introduced computer and Internet education into the primary school curriculum in order to ensure that all students could participate in the new economy sectors if they chose to. Each of these policy solutions had the goal of encouraging entrepreneurship while also limiting its distributional impact on society. And in each of these policy areas, France's solutions have entailed a heightened—rather than diminished—regulatory activism by the state.

France initiated technology policy reforms in response to a perceived failure to commercialize new research findings. Weakness in this area persisted in 2002. One troubling sign was the decreasing level of government R&D spending in France. In 2000, the French government spent 0.93 percent of GDP on R&D, down from 0.97 percent in 1999. This compared poorly with the 1.84 percent of GDP spent by the government on R&D in Britain, 2.46 percent in Germany, and 2.64 in the United States.[3] Moreover, despite government incentives, venture capital investment in France was also smaller than that of its neighbors. Venture capital investment as a percentage of GDP in 2002 was 0.8 percent in Britain, 0.4 percent in Germany, and 0.5 percent in France.[4] Patent applications to the European Patent Office also showed signs that France continued to lag its neighbors, as well as the United States (see table 6-1). And France still lagged in the use of the Internet.

But alongside these troubling aggregate indicators, important changes were nonetheless emerging. Government financing of R&D, though limited, was increasingly finding its way to start-up ventures. France's start-up funds (Fonds d'amorçage) had raised 86.5 million euros and supported 245 new companies in their first three years of existence.[5] France's thirty-one new public incubators had by the end of 2002 supported 550 compa-

Table 6-1. *Patents Filed with the European Patent Office per Million Inhabitants, 2000*

Number of patents

Country	All patents	High-tech patents	Growth in high-tech patents, 1995–2000 (percent)
France	140	27.8	17.4
Germany	170	43.7	26.5
Sweden	346	95.1	29.3
United States	158	49.5	27.2
United Kingdom	124	27.5	18.2

Source: Data from Alice Zoppè, "Patent Activities in the EU: Towards High-Tech Patenting 1990 to 2000," *Science and Technology* (Eurostat), theme 9, no. 1 (2002).

nies with 24.6 million euros.[6] And France's effort to create an environment conducive to venture capital appeared to be enjoying some success. As in other advanced industrial countries, French private equity was hurt by the decline in technology investment beginning in 2000, but three positive trends are worth noting.

First, venture capital investments in France did not fall as sharply as in other countries. France's experience compares favorably to the 27 percent decline in venture capital raised in Europe as a whole (see figure 6-1). The relatively small decline in France has been attributed to FCPI funds, which raised 1.5 billion euros between their creation in 1997 and the beginning of 2002.[7] Because these funds were required to be invested within a two-year window, the FCPI countered the general technology sector downturn. In 2002 they accounted for one third of all venture capital investment in France.[8]

Second, France was able to maintain support for many companies that had already received initial start-up funds. While early-stage investment was curtailed in the economic downturn of 2002, later-stage investment in development and buyouts saw only a small drop. This sustained investment was supported by France's FCPIs, whose investment managers increasingly saw late-stage investments as a less risky investment strategy. And most venture-supported start-ups were still able to find buyers, either through an IPO or a trade sale. In 2001, write-offs represented only 9.5 percent of French venture capital divestment, compared with 31 percent in Britain, 36 percent in Germany, and 54 percent in Sweden.[9]

Figure 6-1.   *Venture Capital Investment as a Percentage of GDP, Country Comparison, 1997–2001*

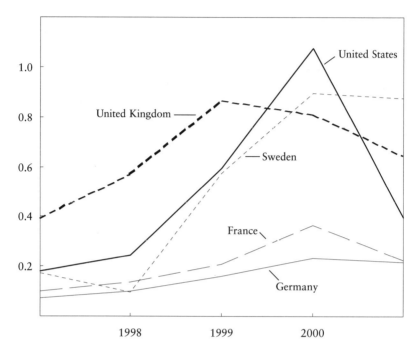

Source: Compiled by author from European Venture Capital Association and National Venture Capital Association data.

The third, and perhaps most important, legacy of the technology bubble of the late 1990s was the new venture capital community that it created in France. In the early 1990s, France had only a small number of successful large venture capital groups: APEX, Sofinnova, and Partech. By 2002, in the wake of the burst technology bubble, venture capital investment had certainly waned. But it left behind a new pool of trained experts in the field. Government-sponsored programs to promote venture investing had given new funds a jump start. France in 2002 enjoyed a pool of technical, financial, and legal expertise that had outlasted the boom-bust technology cycle.

One sign that France had begun to offer a favorable climate for risky investment was an influx of private equity investment from abroad. Foreign investment as a percentage of total private equity investment increased from 22 percent in 1999 to 42 percent in 2000. It fell to 33 percent in

Figure 6-2. *France's Aspiring Entrepreneurs, 1992–2002*

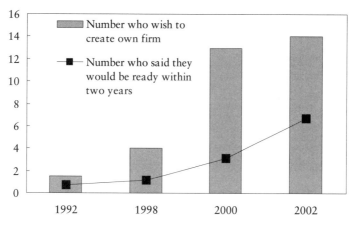

Millions

Source: Ifop survey conducted for the Salon des entrepreneurs and APCE (Agence pour la création d'entreprises). See Pierre Kupferman, "L'Etat doit s'attaquer aux problèmes d'après création," *La Tribune*, January 29, 2002, p. 29; APCE, "Les Français et la création d'entreprise," Press Release, January 21, 2000 [www.apce.com/bar.htm [January 8, 2001]); Ifop, "Les Français et la création d'entreprise" (www.apce.com/chiffres/ifop2000.html [February 5, 2000]); "A la découverte de l'entrepreneur occasionnel," *La Tribune*, January 12, 1998, p. 42.

2001. The absolute volume of foreign investment increased threefold in one year, to 3.2 billion euros in 2000.[10] While the influx of risk capital may have reflected in part the decline in the U.S. technology sector, it also suggested that the French environment for private equity investment was favorable. Partech, a venture capital firm with offices in both the United States and France, reported similar rates of return in both markets (33 percent in the United States, 29 percent in France).[11]

Perhaps the most important change for France during this period was a growing cultural acceptance of entrepreneurship. One sign of this was the dramatic growth in the number of French citizens interested in creating their own companies. This number increased tenfold in the decade ending in 2002. More significantly, the number claiming to be ready to do so within two years also grew. At the beginning of 2002, 6.7 million French over age 18—about 10 percent of the total population—said they were ready to create their own company within two years, up from only 700,000 in 1992 (see figure 6-2).[12] Of course, many of those who did launch technology start-ups in the late 1990s lost their jobs with the collapse of the technology bubble. But even they were likely to remain entrepreneurs, if only because it is difficult in France to reenter traditional career tracks once one has left. As venture capitalist François Véron observed, "Those who participated [in technology start-ups] are either abroad or unemployed. But they are not in France's large corporations."[13]

The cultural transformation would inevitably take longer than six years. Despite the growing interest, skepticism about entrepreneurship in France remained. Laurent Kott, founder of I-Source, noted, "The French still have a sense of *Schadenfreude* when others fail. And when they succeed, their response is to be jealous rather than to copy them."[14] And traditional professions still had allure among the French youth. A January 2001 survey of 18- to 40-year-olds found that 47 percent would prefer to work in the public sector. Of the 51 percent preferring the private sector, 80 percent favored working in a "classic" company; only 18 percent preferred to work in a start-up.[15] Stéphane Boujnah, one of the designers of France's reforms under Jospin, half-joked that most French were glad to see the technology bubble burst, if only so that they would not have to worry anymore about the entrepreneurial culture that it had sponsored.[16]

By the end of 2002, the economic track record of France's experiment with high-tech start-ups remained mixed. In the short term, France's most startling achievement was its ability to make dramatic policy reforms in order to promote domestic competitiveness in the new technology sectors. For better or for worse, France achieved this without undermining traditional functions of the state—in selecting new technologies, in promoting social equality, in setting a regulatory framework for the economy. At the end of 2002, the question remained whether French regulatory reforms would continue to follow a middle road or instead become (as some observers suggested) a Trojan horse for the forces of liberalization. Would regulatory and fiscal reforms enacted with careful attention to their impact on the French social environment evolve eventually into policies of outright deregulation?

Early signs suggested that this outcome was unlikely. On the one hand, France's strongest advocates of entrepreneurship were also vocally critical of the American style of deregulation. The American stock-options regime, in which options were often granted at a discount and with minimal time restrictions on exercising them, was seen by French entrepreneurs to encourage short-termism.[17] French reformers were also skeptical of the U.S. emphasis on private pension funds. Even French venture capitalists worried that American pension funds such as CALpers (the California state retirement fund) were trying to push France to adopt a private pension system primarily so that French retirement savings could help to buoy the U.S. stock market (where much of it would presumably be invested) and thereby support U.S. assets. As one venture capitalist noted, "I don't want France to be paying U.S. pensions."

On the other hand, France still lacked many of the elements that had made the U.S. model successful. Despite efforts at forging a common European market for goods, for example, French venture capitalists were simply not able to scale up new start-ups as fast as they could in the large U.S. market. Nor did France have U.S.-style agencies, such as the National Aeronautics and Space Administration and the National Science Foundation, to channel government funds into peer-reviewed research. Such programs had acted as stabilizers during the U.S. economic downturn in 2000, helping to sustain research projects through a trough in private venture support. The Small Business Administration Act also called on the U.S. government to favor contracts to small businesses. France had not pursued this approach, which appeared in any case to be illegal under European Union competition law. In practice, French government contracts continued to be biased *against* small contractors; large companies were seen as more likely to complete long-term contracts.[18]

Prime Minister Jospin announced in June 1997, "The ambition of my government is to facilitate the development of the information society in France while permitting as many people as possible to gain access to the new services." In this early statement emerged a tension—one that pervaded France's policy toward the Internet and indeed toward economic liberalization in general—between a commitment to dramatic reform and an equal commitment to social solidarity. Policies designed to promote the commercialization of new information and communications technologies balanced the economic reality France faced in competing in new technology sectors against the political and social values that continued to distinguish French from American society. In this sense, the technology policy France put in place between 1996 and 2002 was both boldly new and familiarly French.

Notes

Chapter One

1. "L'innovation en quête d'une dimension européenne," *Les Echos*, December 7, 2000, p. 59.

2. Jean François-Poncet, *Rapport d'information sur l'expatriation des jeunes Français* (Paris: Sénat 388, 2000).

3. Daniel Bell, *The Coming of Post-Industrial Society* (Basic Books, 1973); Lester Thurow, *Building Wealth* (Harper Collins, 1999).

4. Philip Evans and Thomas S. Wurster, *Blown to Bits: How the New Economics of Information Transforms Strategy* (Harvard Business School Press, 2000); Rosabeth Moss Kanter, *E-Volve: Succeeding in the Digital Culture of Tomorrow* (Harvard Business School Press, 2001).

5. Stephen S. Cohen, J. Bradford Delong, Steven Weber, and John Zysman, "Tools: The Drivers of E-Commerce," in *Tracking a Transformation: E-Commerce and the Terms of Competition in Industries* (Brookings 2001), p. 3.

6. Eugen Weber, *Peasants into Frenchmen: The Modernization of Rural France, 1870–1914* (Stanford University Press, 1976), p. 218.

7. Benedict Anderson, *Imagined Communities: Reflections on the Origin and Spread of Nationalism* (Cornell University Press, 1983).

8. Laurent Kott, interview by the author, Paris, October 2002.

9. Debate persists on when and if these state-sponsored projects actually recovered their development costs. Airbus, for example, is notoriously secretive about the development costs for its A300 aircraft. Estimates on the break-even point for the Minitel network differ by as much as fifteen years.

10. Suzanne Berger and Michael J. Piore, *Dualism and Discontinuity in Industrial Societies* (Cambridge University Press, 1980).

11. Andrew Shonfield, *Modern Capitalism: The Changing Balance of Public and Private Power* (Oxford University Press, 1965), p. 138.

12. J. Nicholas Ziegler, *Governing Ideas: Strategies for Innovation in France and Germany* (Cornell University Press, 1997), pp. 28–31.

13. Peter Hall, *Governing the Economy: The Politics of State Intervention in Britain and France* (Oxford University Press, 1986), pp. 189–91.

14. John Zysman, *Political Strategies for Industrial Order: State, Market and Industry in France* (University of California Press, 1977); Elie Cohen, *Le Colbertisme "high-tech": économie des telecom et du grand projet* (Paris: Pluriel, 1992).

15. Jonah Levy, *Tocqueville's Revenge: State, Society, and Economy in Contemporary France* (Harvard University Press, 1999).

16. Christian Sautter, "La volonté de croissance solidaire," *Les Echos*, May 23, 2000, p. 76.

17. Alain Minc, *www.capitalisme.fr* (Paris: Grasset, 2000), p. 210.

18. *Recherche et innovation: la France dans la compétition mondiale*, report of the working group led by Bernard Majoie, Commissariat général du plan, November 1999.

19. Annie Kahn, "La France est dans la course, mais plus en tête," *Le Monde*, November 7, 2000.

20. Virginie Malingre, "Lionel Jospin offert de nouvelles aides aux créateurs d'entreprise," *Le Monde*, April 12, 2000.

21. Philippe Mustar, " Les entreprises créées par des chercheurs, " *Formation par la Recherche* 49 (January 1995).

22. *Tableau de bord de l'innovation* (Paris: Economics Ministry, 1999).

23. Thierry Desjardins, *Arrêtez d'emmerder les français!* (Paris: Plon, 2000), p. 219.

24. Yann Duchesne, "Etats généraux de la création d'entreprises: pour quoi faire?" *Le Monde*, April 11, 2000.

25. Jean Pisani-Ferry, "Les mutations du travail en Europe," *Libération*, October 1, 2001.

26. Interestingly, it is also the logic behind the apparently contradictory thirty-five-hour workweek initiative that was pursued in parallel with efforts to support small-firm dynamism.

27. Godefroy Beauvallet, interview by the author, Paris, October 2002.

28. See Steven K. Vogel, *Freer Markets, More Rules* (Cornell University Press, 1996), pp. 16–19.

29. Benoît Habert, interview by the author, Paris, October 2002.

30. "En 2000, les partenaires sociaux seront consultés en amont des artibrages budgetaires," *Les Echos*, October 12, 1999, p. 4.

31. Laurent Maudui, "Lionel Jospin met en place un conseil d'analyse économique pluraliste," *Le Monde*, July 25, 1997.

32. Emmanuel Lechypre and Marc Landre, "L'Etat aveugle," *L'Expansion*, September 1, 2003, p. 68.

33. Christian Poncelet, president of the French Senate (www.senat.fr/evenement/immersion/index.html).

34. www.senat.fr/evenement/immersion/liste_entreprise.html.

35. Frederic Mauro, economic analyst for the French Sénat, interview by the author, Washington, D.C., Spring 2001.

36. Gaelle Macke, "L'Etat prend le virage de la nouvelle économie," *Le Monde*, June 20, 2001.

37. Etienne Mougeotte, "Dominique Strauss-Kahn ouvert à un statut particulier pour les start-up," *Les Echos*, December 14, 1998.

38. David Owen, "French Push to Boost New Companies," *Financial Times*, July 7, 1999.

39. Odile Renaud, interview by the author, Paris, October 2002.

40. Jean-Noël Tronc, interview by the author, Paris, October 2002.

Chapter Two

1. Stéphane Boujnah, interview by the author, Paris, October 2002; a Finance Ministry official, interview by the author, Paris, October 2002.

2. Stéphane Boujnah, interview.

3. "Discours de Monsieur Jacques Chirac, Président de la République, lors des Premiers Etats Généraux des Jeunes Entrepreneurs Européens," Paris Chamber of Commerce and Industry (www.ccip.fr/dircom/dis-jchirac.htm [February 22, 2001]).

4. John Ardagh, *France Today* (Penguin, 1982), p. 39.

5. Ifop, "Les Français et la création d'entreprise" (www.apce.com/chiffres/ifop2000.html [February 5, 2000]).

6. APCE, "Les Français et la création d'entreprise," press release, January 21, 2000 (www.apce.com/bar.htm [January 8, 2001]).

7. Michel Meyer, interview by the author, Paris, October 2002.

8. Jean-François Poncet, *Rapport d'information sur l'expatriation des jeunes Français* (Paris: Sénat 338, June 7, 2000), pp. 9–10, quotation on p. 19.

9. Cited in Thierry Desjardins, *Arrêtez d'emmerder les Français!* (Paris: Plon, 2000), p. 226.

10. Ifop, "Les 18–40 Ans, le travail et l'entreprise de leur rêve," APCE, January 18, 2000 (www.apce.com/chiffres/ifop2001/ifop2001.html [February 5, 2001]).

11. David S. Landes, "French Entrepreneurship and Industrial Growth in the Nineteenth Century," *Journal of Economic History*, vol. 9 (May 1949), p. 56.

12. APCE, CDC, and BDPME (APCE, Caisse des Dépôts et Consignations, and Banque du Développement des Petites et Moyennes Entreprises), "Le Financement des plus petites créations d'entreprises: enquête," November 2000, p. 6 (www.apce.com/upload/fishiers/observatoire/etudes/enquetefinancement.pdf).

13. Yann Duchesne, "Etats généraux de la création d'entreprises: pour quoi faire?" *Le Monde*, April 11, 2000.

14. Francine Aizicovici, "Les idées ne manquent pas pour dynamiser la création d'entreprises," *Le Monde*, March 10, 1998.

15. APCE, "Start-up en France, des mythes aux réalités," June 14, 2000, p. 50 (www.apce.com/upload/ouvrage/startup.pdf).

16. Kevin J. Delaney and David Wessel, "Lack of Options Tempers Europe's High-Tech Startups," *Wall Street Journal Interactive Edition* (www.startup.wsj.com/n/SB945872196119013808-regional-profiles.html [January 16, 2001]).

17. Law 70-1322, December 31, 1970; Jean-Baptiste Jacquin, Franck Dedieu, and Didier Rossignol, "Nouvelles fortunes, nouvelles moeurs," *L'Expansion*, September 14, 2000 (www.lexpansion.com [January 8, 2000]).

18. "Stock-options: évolution de la fiscalité," AILES (Aide et informations à l'usage des embauchés sorties de L'ESIAL) (dchaffiol.free.fr/infogene/argent/ stocksOptions/art_SOevolFisc.htm [December 2000]).

19. Under this scheme, stock options had to be held for at least five years to receive the 33.5 percent tax rate; further value added was taxed at the standard 19.4 percent rate. Because of the five-year holding rule, the fiscal benefits of this new tax regime began to be felt only in 2000. Arnaud Leparmentier, "Les bases d'imposition de l'épargne sont élargies pour taxer l'argent qui dort," *Le Monde*, September 22, 1995.

20. Sophie Péters Van Deinse, "Une loi pour moraliser les stock options," *L'Usine Nouvelle*, July 13, 1995.

21. Pierre Angel Gay, "Les patrons sont-ils trop payés?" *Le Monde*, September 6, 1994; Erich Inciyan, "La mise en examen du PDG d'Alcatel-Alsthom," *Le Monde*, July 8, 1994.

22. Robert Graham, "The Soft-Option," *Financial Times*, April 28, 2000, p. 18.

23. Antoine Décitre, interview by the author, Paris, October 2002.

24. Benoît Habert, interview by the author, Paris, October 2002.

25. Michel Meyer, interview by the author, Paris, October 2002.

26. Ivan Best, "Le gouvernement compte baisser la taxation des stock-options de 40 a 26%," *La Tribune*, December 16, 1998, p. 4.

27. "Des arbitrages significatifs sur les dossiers sensibles," *Le Monde*, July 11, 2000; Pierre Le Hir, "La loi sur l'innovation a pour objet la création de plusieurs milliers d'emplois," *Le Monde*, January 14, 1999.

28. Jacquin, Dedieu, and Rossignol, "Nouvelles fortunes."

29. Déminor, "2000 Déminor Rating Press Release," December 2000 (www.deminor.com [December 19, 2000]).

30. Samer Iskandar, "Change Has Come Swiftly," *Financial Times*, March 19, 1999, p. 2.

31. Graham, "The Soft-Option"; "The Strike Threatens Philippe Jaffré," *Challenges* (June 1999) (www.perso.wanadoo.fr/elf-resistance/presse/challenges 9906eng.htm [January 16, 2001]).

32. Stéphane Boujnah, interview.

33. Henri Emmanuelli, interview by *Nouvel Économiste* (April 21–May 4, 2000); Laurent Mauduit, "Laurent Fabius à la recherche d'un compromis dur les stock-options," *Le Monde*, April 25, 2000.

34. Fanny Beuscart, "Rémunération des dirigeant: les stock-options en mal de réforme," *L'Usine Nouvelle*, October 21, 1999.

35. Virginie Malingre and Michel Noblecourt, "Les députés PS veulent taxes davantage les stock-options," *Le Monde*, October 15, 1999.

36. Stéphane Boujnah, interview.

37. www.myweb.worldnet.net/~chiffres/infogene/argent/stocksOptions/art_SoevolFisc.htm (December 20, 2000).

38. Ibid.

39. Fanny Beuscart, "Stock-options: rien n'est réglé," *L'Usine Nouvelle*, May 4, 2000.

40. See Brian Hall, "What You Need to Know about Stock Options," *Harvard Business Review* (March–April 2000), p. 122.

41. Jacquin, Dedieu, and Rossignol, "Nouvelles fortunes."

42. Graham, "The Soft-Option."

43. Jean-Léon Vandoorne, "Stock-options: les Français convertis," *L'Usine Nouvelle*, July 13, 2000.

44. Jacqueline Mattei and Jean-Christophe Féraud, "Philippe Jaffré, l'inspecteur des cyberfinances," *L'Expansion*, December 21, 2000 (www.lexpansion.com [January 8, 2001]).

45. "Taux de diffusion par entreprise" (www.stock-option.fr/html/palmares.asp [Jan. 9, 2000]).

46. Vandoorne, "Stock-options."

47. Organization for Economic Cooperation and Development (OECD), *Economic Survey: France* (Paris: OECD, 2000), p. 89.

48. Yann Duchesne, "Etats généraux de la création d'entreprises: pour quoi faire?" *Le Monde*, April 11, 2000.

49. Cited in *The Economist*, July 8, 2000, pp. 50–51.

50. Commission of the European Union, *Benchmarking Enterprise Policy: First Results from the Scoreboard*, SEC no. 1841 (Brussels, October 27, 2000), p. 38.

51. Quoted in Desjardins, *Arrêtez d'emmerder les Français*.

52. Cécile Cornudet, "Le gouvernement annonce des mésures pour simplifier les formalités des PME," *Les Echos*, December 4, 1997, p. 4.

53. Net-Enterprises, *Actualités* (www.portail.net-entreprises.fr/actu/jactu.htm [December 13, 2000]).

54. Xavier Gueroux, "Les salariés ont une bonne image des chefs d'entreprise," *Canal-Ipsos*, October 28, 1998 (www.ipsos.fr/CanalIpsos/articles/251.asp?rubld=251).

55. Jean-Marie Bockel, Philippe Rouvillois, and Laurent Degroote, "Rapport sur la simplification de la création d'entreprise, de la vie des créateurs et de la gestion de leurs entreprises," January 23, 2001 (www.ladocfrancaise.gouv.fr/fic_pdf/bockel.pdf [January 8, 2000)]), p. 43.

56. Jean François-Poncet, *L'Expatriation des jeunes Français*, Senate Report 388, June 7, 2000, pp. 48–50.

57. Marie-laure Cittanova, "La loi Madelin assouplit le statut des entrepreneurs individuels," *Les Echos*, January 17, 1994, p 3.

58. Virginie Malingre, "Lionel Jospin offre de nouvelles aides aux créateurs d'entreprise," *Le Monde*, April 12, 2000.

59. "Ces petites simplifications qui changent la vie," *Les Echos*, August 11, 2000, p. 2.

60. Geoffroy Larany, "Créateurs d'entreprise: ce que l'Etat fait pour vous," *Creascopie*, September 21, 2000 (www.creascope.net/contenu/creascopie/1109.phtml [December 13, 2000]).

61. Bockel, Rouvillois, and Degroote, "Rapport sur la simplification de la création d'entreprise."

62. Cornudet, "Le gouvernement annonce des mésures pour simplifier les formalités des PME."

63. Godefroy Beauvallet, interview by the author, Paris, October 2002.

64. Office of the e-Envoy, "Benchmarking Electronic Service Delivery," April 21, 2000 (www.e-envoy.gov.uk/2000/reports.htm [February 6, 2000]).

65. Dan Lerner, "Government Services Slow to Go Online," *Financial Times*, June 5, 2000, p. 14.

66. Jean-Noël Tronc, interview by the author, Paris, October 2002.

67. Larany, "Créateurs d'entreprise."

68. "La nouvelle société par actions simplifiée," *Le Moniteur des travaux publics et du bâtiment* (April 21, 2000), p. 104.

69. Jean Thibaud, "Overthrow of Ancien Regime," *Financial Times*, March 8, 1994, p. 18.

70. "Loi no 99-587 du 12 juillet 1999 sur l'innovation et la recherche," *Le Journal Officiel: Lois et Décrets* (July 13, 1999), p. 10396.

71. "Réforme de la société par actions simplifiée (SAS): une nouvelle structure pour les PME et les personnes physiques," *Le Nouveau Courrier*, Magazine of the Chamber of Commerce and Industry of Paris (www.ccip.fr/dircom/nouveaucourrier/nc-juridhtml [November 29, 2000]).

72. Etienne Mougeotte, "Les patrons français de la Silicon Valley ont réuni a Bercy et a Nantes un millier d'élèves des grandes écoles pour les persuader de devenir entrepreneurs," *Les Echos*, December 14, 1998, p. 21.

73. Ibid.

74. "Réforme de la société par actions simplifiée."

75. Ibid.

76. This is not allowed by the EURL, a form of the SARL company format that applies specifically to single-owner companies.

77. Cécile Desjardins, "La SAS, nouvelle structure privilégiée des start-up," *Les Echos*, March 1, 2000, p. 58.

78. Antoine Décitre, interview.

79. Olivier Protard, interview by the author, Paris, October 2002.

80. Jean-Marie Rausch, *Research*, vol. 7 of the *Projet de loi de finances pour 2001*, Sénat, no. 94, November 23, 2000, pp. 28, 30, 33 (www.senat.fr/rap/a00-094-7/a00-094-71.pdf).

81. Alain Pérez, "Innovation: le projet de loi vise à encourager la création d'entreprises par des chercheurs," *Les Echos*, January 14, 1999.

82. Arthur Andersen and APCE, "Du Créateur d'entreprise au créateur d'emplois: La dynamique du success," January 1998, p. 31 (www.autocupacio.org/ese/createur.pdf).

83. David Owen, "French Push to Boost New Companies," *Financial Times*, July 7, 1999.

84. Antoine Reverchon, "Les régions de la matière grise," *Le Monde*, March 6, 2001.

85. Pierre Lafitte, *Projet de loi de finances pour 2002, Tome VIII: Recherche scientifique et technique* (Paris: Sénat, 2001).

86. Laurent Kott, interview by the author, Paris, October 2002.

87. Alain Costes, "Les Réseaux de recherche et d'innovation technologiques, Bilan au 31 décembre 2002," Ministère délégué à la recherche et aux nouvelles technologies, April 2003.

88. Laurent Kott, interview.

89. Sophia-Antipolis (www.sophia-antipolis.net/infos/frame.htm); Geof Wheelright, "Tale of Two Internets," *Financial Post*, August 16, 1997, section 3, p. 29.

90. "Biotechnologies et mobiles au secours de Sophia-Antipolis," *Les Echos*, November 26, 2001.

91. Mick Mumford, "Technopoles, Politics and Markets," in Margaret Sharp and Peter Holmes, eds., *Strategies for New Technology: Case Studies from Britain and France* (New York: Philip Allan, 1989), pp. 88–89.

92. Antoine Reverchon, "C'est une erreur de suspendre l'effort de recherche parce qu'une technologie est en crise, " *Le Monde*, September 11, 2001.

93. Quoted in Reverchon, "Les régions de la matière grise."

94. Philippe Collombel, interview by the author, Paris, October 2002.

95. Nicholas Véron, interview by the author, Paris, October 2002.

Chapter Three

1. Michel Meyer, interview by the author, Paris, October 2002.

2. Jean-Jacques Salomon, *Le Gaulois, le cowboy, et le samouraï: la politique française de la technologie* (Paris: Economica, 1986), p. 139.

3. Hervé Ponchelet, "Les locomotives de l'innovation," *Le Point*, May 10, 1996.

4. Stéphane Boujnah, interview by the author, Paris, October 2002.

5. Commission of the European Union, *Benchmarking Enterprise Policy: First Results from the Scoreboard*, SEC no. 1841 (Brussels, October 27, 2000), pp. 17–18.

6. "Record Levels Invested and Raised in 2000," EVCA press release, Rome, June 14, 2001; Venture Economics (www.ventureeconomics.com); European Venture Capital Association, *EVCA Yearbook* (Brussels: EVCA, 2001), pp. 131, 133.

7. Cécile Prudhomme and Enguerand Renauld, "Internet, nouvel eldorado de l'économie française," *Le Monde*, March 20, 2000; "Financement: 2001, année de la rationalization et de la consolidation," *Journal du Net*, December 26, 2001.

8. In Sweden, the pension fund share of VC fell to 18.3 percent in 2001. In France it fell to 6.9 percent. In Britain it increased to 42.2 percent (*EVCA Yearbook*, pp. 230, 248); a 1979 change to the U.S. Employee Retirement Income

Security Act (ERISA) allowed private pensions to invest in private capital, driving strong growth in venture capital investment. Sweden similarly opened its pension funds to VC in 1994.

9. The French system is administered jointly by France's employers' association, Medef, and France's large labor unions. It is also a complex, fragmented system of supports, comprising a range of different funds targeting different professions and income levels.

10. Bruno Palier, "Pension Reform in France: An Issue 'Sans Issue'?" paper presented at the Center for European Studies, Harvard University, December 4, 2001.

11. John Ardagh, *France in the New Century: Portrait of a Changing Society* (London: Penguin, 2000).

12. Jean François-Poncet, *La fuite des cerveaux: mythe ou réalité?* Rapport d'information 388 (1999–2000).

13. Cited in "Déception parmi les créateurs de start-up," *Les Echos*, April 12, 2000, p. 3.

14. Government official, interview by the author, Paris, October 2002.

15. Stéphane Boujnah, interview.

16. Contributions to unemployment insurance, pensions, and worker disability are collected separately from government taxes. They are so-called "social contributions" and go into funds that are comanaged by organizations that represent management and labor.

17. Véronique Dupont, "L'engouement pour la technologie dope les FCPI," *Le Monde*, March 6, 2000.

18. Gaelle Macke, "L'Etat prend le virage de la nouvelle économie," *Le Monde*, June 20, 2001.

19. René Trégrouët, *Projet de loi sur l'innovation et la recherche*, Sénat, Finance Commission, Opinion 210 (98–99).

20. "L'Agence de l'innovation fait du neuf depuis vingt ans," *Le Monde*, November 3, 1999; Denis, "Vingt ans de soutien aux PME."

21. Macke, "L'Etat prend le virage."

22. Denis, "Vingt ans de soutien aux PME"; ANVAR, *Rapport d'Activité 2000* (Paris: ANVAR, 2001).

23. Macke, "L'Etat prend le virage."

24. Denis, "Vingt ans de soutien aux PME."

25. "ANVAR, Historique: Innovation Vocation, 1979–1999" (www.anvar.fr).

26. "L'Anvar veut accentuer son influence financière sur les PME," *Les Echos*, January 26, 1998, p. 14.

27. Macke, "L'Etat prend le virage."

28. Laurence Imbert, "L'Anvar donnera un coup de pouce aux services Web," *01Net*, May 10, 2000 (www.01net.com [January 3, 2001]).

29. Fabrice Cavarretta, interview by the author, Paris, October 2002.

30. Michel Meyer, interview by the author, Paris, October 2002.

31. Benoît Habert, interview by the author, Paris, October 2002.

32. "Des montants multipliés par dix en cinq ans," *La Tribune*, April 28, 1999, p. 16.

33. Bernard Le Court, "Investir dans des sociétés innovantes via des FCPI permet des réductions d'impôts," *Le Monde*, November 23, 1998.

34. "Une réforme de la réglementation des FCPI devrait entrer en vigueur début 2002," *Les Echos*, July 20, 2001; "Capital-risque: les FCPI et l'Etat font l'appoint en France," *Les Echos*, April 29, 2002, p. 102.

35. "Les avantages des FCPI prolonges," *Le Monde*, December 11, 2000.

36. Philippe Collombel, interview by the author, Paris, October 2002.

37. "Les professionnels critiquent un corpus réglementaire trop pesant," *Les Echos*, July 20, 2001.

38. François Véron, interview by the author, Paris, October 2002.

39. "The French Government Is Making Life Harder for Employers," *Economist*, June 16, 2001.

40. APCE, "Start-up en France, des mythes aux réalités," June 14, 2000, p. 50 (Paris: Agence pour la création d'entreprises).

41. Sylvie Cieply, "Bridging Capital Gaps to Promote Innovation in France," *Industry and Innovation*, vol. 8, no. 2 (2001), pp. 173–75.

42. Macke, "L'Etat prend le virage."

43. "Observatoire de la stratégie de placement des ménages français," *Taylor-Nelson Sofres*, December 16, 1999 (www.sofres.com/compress/compress_content.asp?ID=45).

44. Patrick Branthomme, "Les comptes financiers de la nation en 2000," *INSEE Première* 779 (May 2001), p. 4.

45. Cieply, "Bridging Capital Gaps," p. 174.

46. *Journal Officiel*, December 31, 1999; "Contrats DSK: la nouvelle génération," *Les Echos*, March 10, 2000, p. 57.

47. Catherine Ducruet, "La France accélère le pas," *Les Echos*, October 18, 2000, p. 65.

48. "Air Liquide Ventures souhaite réaliser une douzaine d'investissements par an," *l'AGEFI*, November 2, 2001, p. 27.

49. Catherine Ducruet, "Air Liquide découvre les charmes du capital-risque," *Les Echos*, October 18, 2000, p. 65.

50. "Le ministre de la high-tech," *Les Echos*, November 3, 1999, p. 6.

51. The flotation was also intended to make possible a stock swap with Deutsche Telekom, but this proposal was blocked under EU competition law.

52. Venture capital firms to receive the FPCR include Aurigass, Sofinnova Capital, Galileo, Siparex, and Banexi Ventures; Macke, "L'Etat prend le virage."

53. Odile Renaud, interview by the author, October 2002.

54. "Laurent Fabius donne naissance au second fonds public en faveur des entreprises innovantes," *Les Echos*, July 20, 2000.

55. Philippe Albert, "Espèces d'incubateurs," *Les Echos*, December 13, 2000, p. 73.

56. Le projet de budget civil de recherche et développement BCRD 2002, p. 23 (www.recherche.gouv.fr/discours/2001/budget/bcrd.pdf).

57. "Projet de loi des financies pour 2001: état de la recherche et du développement technologique," p. 97 (www.recherche.gouv.fr/recherche/finance/chiffresb.htm).

58. Severine Ghys, "Les incubateurs de la net économie s'auto-analysent," *ZDNet.fr*, December 14, 2000 (www.news.zdnet.fr/story/0,,t118-s2061860,00.html).

59. "Les difficultés des start-up mettent les incubateurs sous pression," *Les Echos*, October 30, 2000, p. 115.

60. "Avec Venturepark, Pixelpark joue la carte de l'incubation en Europe," *Les Echos*, December 4, 2000, p. 119.

61. "Un Incubateur de sociétés de biotech crée à l'institut Pasteur," *La Tribune*, December 11, 2000.

62. www.tocamak.com/en/frm_en.htm [January 3, 2001]).

63. "Startup Avenue parie sur l'essaimage des grands comptes," *Les Echos*, December 18, 2000, p. 113.

64. "Le Social fait son entrée dans les 'start-up,'" *La Croix*, January 3, 2001, p. 4.

65. Antoine Décitre, interview by the author, October 2002.

66. Macke, "L'Etat prend le virage." "

67. "Le Ministère de la recherche satisfait du premier bilan des incubateurs," *La Tribune*, July 10, 2001.

68. Ducruet, "La France accélère le pas."

69. Alain Perez, "Le Rapport Guillaume: un requisitoire pour la filière innovation en France," *Les Echos*, March 13, 1998.

70. "L'amélioration du cadre juridique et fiscal ne supprime pas le retard français," *Les Echos*, March 1, 2000, p. 58; Pierre Kupferman, "La Caisse des dépôts veut renforcer son aide aux PME," *La Tribune*, June 23, 2000, p. 34.

71. Macke, "L'Etat prend le virage"; Jérôme Batteau, "Amorçage, mode d'emploi," *JDNet*, November 7, 2001 (www.journaldunet.com/dossiers/krisk/amorcage/lesfonds.shtml).

72. *JDNet*, November 7, 2001 (www.journaldunet.com/dossiers/krisk/amorcage/etat.shtml).

73. Roger-Gérard Schwartzenberg, speech on the occasion of the creation of the Comité Consultatif du Développement Technologique, April 12, 2001 (www.recherche.gouv.fr/discours/2001/dccdt.htm).

74. Paul Molga, "L'Etat injecte 5 milliards de francs dans les PMI innovantes," *Les Echos*, March 24, 1999.

75. Ducruet, "La France accélère le pas."

76. www.recherche.gouv.fr/technologie/concours/.

77. Speech by Roger-Gérard Schwartzenberg, La Sorbonne, September 17, 2001 (www.recherche.gouv.fr/technologie/concours/default.htm).

78. www.tremplin-entreprises.senat.fr/avantages.html.

79. Jean-Marie Bockel, *Le Financement de la création d'entreprise*, Report to the Prime Minister, January 23, 2001, p. 8.

80. Stéphane Boujnah, interview.

Chapter Four

1. Ross Tieman, "Minitel Millions Enticed by Web," *Financial Times*, June 9, 1999, p. 12; *Computer Industry Almanac* (www.c-i-a.com/200103iu.htm [May 7, 2001]); www.nua.ie/surveys/how_many_online/europe.html.

2. Respondents are age 16 and older; positive responses included Internet access either at home or at work. *Computer Industry Almanac* (www.c-i-a.com/200103iu.htm [May 7, 2001]).

3. www.nua.ie/surveys/how_many_online.

4. *Enarques* are graduates of ENA, l'Ecole Nationale d'Administration; *agrégés* are professors. Guy Sorman, "Pourquoi les Français rechignent a prendre le virage de la 'nouvelle révolution scientifique,'" *Le Figaro*, February 10, 2001.

5. Cited in Adam Sage, "Why Citizen Citroën Won't Surf," *New Statesman* (December 18, 2000).

6. Paul-André Tavoillot, "L'entrée dans l'ère de l'information, priorité nationale?" *La Tribune*, March 24, 1997, p. 25.

7. Cited in Gail Edmondson, "A French Internet Revolution?" *Business Week*, September 29, 1997.

8. Joseph A. Schumpeter, *Capitalism, Socialism and Democracy* (New York: Harper and Row, 1952), p. 140; see also Clayton Christensen, *The Innovator's Dilemma* (Boston: Harvard Business School Press, 1997), p. 15.

9. Interestingly, the growth trend in Internet access for all countries was largely linear over this period. This finding contradicts the central expectation of network theory, a body of economic literature predicting that network technologies will grow unevenly. With few users, networks should spread slowly, until they reach a critical mass or tipping point, at which the benefits of the network grow rapidly and draw in increasing numbers of users. This expectation is based on the idea that bigger networks are better. The theory has been confirmed for the spread of ATMs, for which "The value of participating for each individual or firm increases with network size." Strikingly, Internet penetration appears not to respond to this endogenous theory of growth. See, for example, Garth Saloner and Andrea Shepard, "Adoption of Technologies with Network Effects: An Empirical Examination of the Adoption of Automated Teller Machines," *The RAND Journal of Economics* (Autumn 1995), pp. 479–501.

10. *OECD Economic Outlook* 67 (June 2000), p. 198.

11. Vivien Schmidt, *From State to Market: The Transformation of French Business and Government* (Cambridge University Press, 1996).

12. Robert Hancke, *Large Firms and Institutional Change: Industrial Renewal and Economic Restructuring in France* (Oxford University Press, 2002).

13. J. Nicholas Ziegler, *Governing Ideas: Strategies for Innovation in France and Germany* (Cornell University Press, 1997), p. 88.

14. Quoted in David Owen, "All Eyes on the Internet," *Financial Times,* November 18, 1998, p. 12.

15. Stéphane Mandard, "Le nouveau eldorado politique," *Le Monde*, November 29, 2000.

16. Cited in ibid.

17. Muriel Humbertjean, "Les Français et l'Internet," *Taylor-Nelson Sofres*, March 2002 (www.sofres.com/etudes/corporate/280302_inernet.htm).

18. Hervé Morin, "Le fossé numérique se creuse entre les internautes et les autres," *Le Monde*, February 1, 2001.

19. Florence Amalou, "La reduction du fossé numérique devient une priorité gouvernementale," *Le Monde*, Communication, July 12, 2000.

20. Jean-Paul de Gaudemar, "Brevet informatique et Internet (b2i) école – collège," *Bulletin Officiel du ministère de l'Education Nationale et du ministère de la Recherche*, no. 42, November 23, 2000.

21. Ibid.

22. "Bilan de trois ans d'action gouvernementale (1998–2000)," *Le Monde*, Communication, July 12, 2001.

23. "L'Internet au programme," *Les Echos*, March 11, 2002, p. 114.

24. Michel Samson, "Lionel Jospin affiche son intérêt pour les technologies de l'information," *Le Monde*, May 17, 2000.

25. Jean-Paul de Gaudemar, "Brevet informatique et Internet (B2i) formation continue—GRETA," *Bulletin Officiel du ministère de l'Education Nationale et du ministère de la Recherche*, no. 31, August 30, 2001.

26. *Bulletin officiel du ministère de l'Education nationale*, no. 31, July 27, 2001.

27. OECD, *Local Access Pricing and E-Commerce*, Report of the Working Party on Telecommunications and Information Services Policies (Paris: OECD, 2000).

28. "Comment démocratiser immédiatement Internet en France?" *Le Figaro*, February 28, 2001.

29. Kristi Essick, "France Fêtes the Internet, but ISPs Are Party Poopers," *Standard*, Europe, March 2, 2001.

30. Olivier Le Quézourec, "Le catalogue d'interconnexion de France Télécom approuvé par l'ART," VNUNet.fr, November 29, 2002.

31. Antoine Reverchon, "La France tarde a faire émerger une stratégie d'amenagement local," *Le Monde*, January 9, 2001.

32. ADSL stands for "asynchronous digital subscriber line." Victoria Shannon, "Updating France," *International Herald Tribune*, July 10, 2001.

33. Guillaume Grallet, "La concurrence gagne le téléphone local," *L'Express*, February 17, 2001 (www.lexpress.fr).

34. A France Télécom official, interview by the author, Paris, October 2002.

35. Another study reports that 35 million users each year use 25,000 different services on Minitel. See Andrew Jack, *The French Exception: Still So Special?* (London: Profile Books, 2000), p. 99; INRIA, *Measuring Information Society*, Eurobarometer 50.1, March 16, 1999, p. 13; Geof Wheelright, "Tale of Two Internets," *Financial Post*, August 16, 1997, section 3, p. 29.

36. Morin, "Le fossé numérique."

37. Yves Mamou, "Le Minitel résiste encore," *Le Monde*, January 9, 2001.

38. Syndicat des entreprises de vente par correspondance et à distance (www.quidfrance.com/WEB/COMMERCE/Q048210.HTM [August 8, 2001]).

39. Tieman, "Minitel Millions Enticed by Web."

40. Mamou, "Le Minitel résiste encore."

41. "La Redoute: un savoir-faire informatique de quarante ans," *Le Monde Informatique 2000* (Paris: IDG France, 2000) (www.weblmi.com/A2000/ENTREP/834_088distributiondel00.htm [September 7, 2001]).

42. Mamou, "Le Minitel résiste encore."

43. Ross Tieman, "Older Technology Helps Jump-Start the Internet Boom," *Financial Times*, December 6, 2000, p. 7; Kenneth Hart, "France Télécom Puts Its Stamp on Internet Market," *Communications Week International*, no. 158, February 5, 1996 (www.totaltele.com/cwi/158news7.html [July 18, 2001]); Samer Iskander, "Minitel Proves a Mixed Blessing," *Financial Times*, February 8, 2000, p. 18.

44. Jack, *The French Exception*, p. 100.

45. Kim Thomas, "Keyed Up and Ready for Battle," *Financial Times*, August 20, 1996, p. 9.

46. Peter Truell, "Follow the French," *Wall Street Journal*, November 14, 1994, section R, p. 35; Polly Sprenger, "Europe: The French Paradox," *Standard*, February 7, 2000; Brad Spurgeon, "Minitel Hangs On in Internet Age," *International Herald Tribune*, March 12, 2001, p. 19.

47. This software created a text window that emulated the Minitel interface, allowing users to access all Minitel features from their own computers. Mamou, "Le Minitel résiste encore."

48. Spurgeon, "Minitel Hangs On in Internet Age."

49. "Internet n'a pas mis le Minitel au Placard," *La Tribune*, April 5, 2001, p. 17.

50. Calculations are based on the number cited in the previous paragraph. Despite their different estimates for Internet and Minitel, the combined calculation is almost the same.

51. INRIA, *Measuring Information Society*, pp. 24–25.

52. Tieman, "Older Technology Helps Jump-Start the Internet Boom,"

53. Philip Gordon and Sophie Meunier, *The French Challenge: Adapting to Globalization* (Washington: Brookings, 2001), p. 4.

54. Jean-Pierre Ponssard, "Stock Options and Performance-Based Pay in France," *U.S.-France Analysis* (Washington: Brookings, March 2001.

55. Thierry Gadault, "Quatre ans pour ouvrir le capital de France Télécom," *La Tribune*, October 24, 1997.

56. Wheelwright, "Tale of Two Internets."

57. "France Télécom lance Wanadoo en Bourse," *L'Express*, July 20, 2001 (www.lexpress.fr [July 20, 2001]).

58. James Connell, "Wanadoo's Parentage Gives It an Edge," *International Herald Tribune*, January 8, 2001, p. 15.

59. Philippe Escande, interview by Elie Cohen, *Les Echos*, January 7, 1998.

60. Connell, "Wanadoo's Parentage Gives it an Edge."

61. Owen, "All Eyes on the Internet."

62. Fabrice Cavarretta, interview by the author, Paris, October 2002.

63. Jeoffrey Nairn, "Search Begins for Internet Successor to Minitel Service," *Financial Times*, October 8, 1999, p. 14.

64. Spurgeon, "Minitel Hangs On in Internet Age"; Philippe Mathonnet and Daniel Kaplan, "E-Commerce Scoreboard Update," Ministry of Finance, September 2002, p. 9 (www.men.minefi.gouv.fr/webmen/informations/tabord/tabord091202_gb.pdf).

65. Spurgeon, "Minitel Hangs On in Internet Age."

66. Iskander, "Minitel Proves a Mixed Blessing."

67. Gérald Bouchez, "La réussite de la banque en ligne passe par le Minitel, selon Forrester," *Le Nouvel Hebdo*, August 3, 2001 (www.01net.com).

68. Dermot McGrath, "Minitel: The Old New Thing," *Wired News*, April 18, 2001 (www.wired.com/news/technology/1,1282,42943,00html [July 31, 2001]).

69. Spurgeon, "Minitel Hangs On in Internet Age."

70. Stephanie Stoll, "Next Click, France," *Guardian*, September 7, 2000, p. 7.

71. Polly Sprenger, "Europe: The French Paradox," *Standard*, February 7, 2000.

72. Pierre Agède, "Au secours, le Minitel revient," *Le Nouvel Hebdo*, January 25, 2001 (www.01net.com); Sprenger, "Europe: The French Paradox."

73. Jean-Noël Tronc, interview by the author, Paris, October 2002.

74. Guy Carrèrre, interview by the author, Paris, October 2002.

75. Michel Alberganti, "Le Minitel pourrait obtenir un sursis grace a son systeme de facturation, " *Le Monde*, August 30, 1997.

76. Spurgeon, "Minitel Hangs On in Internet Age."

77. "L'inspection des finances en ligne," *Le Monde*, March 3, 2001.

78. Guy Carrèrre, interview.

79. Iskander, "Minitel Proves a Mixed Blessing."

80. *Les Echos*, June 25, 1999.

81. "Alcatel Claims Internet First," *Financial Times*, October 26, 1999, p. 23.

82. Owen, "All Eyes on the Internet."

83. Philippe Escande, "France Télécom et IBM s'allient pour démocratiser l'acces a Internet," *Les Echos*, October 7, 1998.

84. Tieman, "Minitel Millions Enticed by Web."

85. Nairn, "Search Begins for Internet Successor.

86. McGrath, "Minitel: The Old New Thing."

87. Nairn, "Search Begins for Internet Successor"; "Atlinks a pris 13% du marche des telephones domestiques," *La Tribune*, March 28, 2001, p. 22.

88. Iskander, "Minitel Proves a Mixed Blessing."

89. Sprenger, "Europe: The French Paradox."

90. EOS Gallup Europe, Eurobarometer 97, February 2001 (http://europa.eu.int/information_society/eeurope/benchmarking/list/source_data_pdf/tables_by_ms.doc).

91. Quid France, "Vente par correspondance et à distance" (www.quidfrance.com/web/commerce/q048210.htm [August 8, 2001]).

92. Spurgeon, "Minitel Hangs On in Internet Age."

Chapter Five

1. Erik Bleich, "Race Policy in France," *US-France Analysis*, May 2001 (www.brook.edu/fp/cusf/analysis/race.htm); Robert Menard, "Liberté de paroles, liberté sur le Net," *Libération*, November 23, 2000, p. 8.

2. Ariana Eunjung Cha, "Rise of Internet 'Borders' Prompts Fears for Web's Future," *Washington Post*, January 4, 2002.

3. Pereira Acacio, "Yahoo condamné a empêcher d'accès des internautes français aux sites illégaux," *Le Monde*, November 22, 2000.

4. Isabelle Repiton, "Les perquisitions et les enquêtes se multiplient autour de Yahoo!" *La Tribune*, November 29, 2000, p. 26.

5. "Germany: Won't sue Yahoo! over 'Mein Kampf,'" *ZDNet UK*, March 22, 2001 (www.news.zdnet.co.uk/story/0,,s2085192,00.html) [June 18, 2001]).

6. Repiton, "Les perquisitions et les enquêtes se multiplient."

7. Thibault Verbiest, "Internet: loi applicable et juridiction compétente," *L'Echo*, November 16, 2000, p. 16.

8. Jean Eaglesham, "A Lost Connection," *Financial Times*, November 21, 2000, p. 28.

9. Lee Dembart, "Yahoo's Surrender," *International Herald Tribune*, January 15, 2001, p. 15.

10. "Site d'enchères nazis: le juge se prononce lundi sur la technique de filtrage," *Agence France-Presse*, November 18, 2000.

11. Cited in Victoria Shannon, "From France, Yahoo Case Resonates around the Globe," *International Herald Tribune*, November 22, 2000; Ben Laurie, "An Expert's Apology," November 21, 2001 (http://www.apache-ssl.org/apology.html).

12. Acacio, "Yahoo condamné a empêcher d'accès des internautes français."

13. Jeff Belle, "The Salt Lake Scramble: Online Coverage of the Olympics," *EContent* (February 2002).

14. Verbiest, "Internet."

15. Jean Eaglesham, "Yahoo! Yields to Ruling by French Court," *Financial Times*, January 4, 2001.

16. Cited in "Putting It in Its Place," *Economist*, August 11, 2001.

17. "Chirac demande un cadre juridique international," *Agence France-Presse*, January 11, 2001.

18. Jacques Attali, interview by Laurent Mauriac and Nicole Pénicault, *Libération*, May 5, 2000.

19. Godefroy Beauvallet, interview by the author, Paris, October 2002.

20. Jean-Noël Tronc, interview by the author, Paris, October 2002.

21. By the end of 2002 the draft law had still not been adopted.

22. Régis Jamin, Philippe Jourdan, Pascal Viguié, *Le Contenu sur le Net: qui droit maîtriser quoi?* Report of the Club.Senat.fr (Paris: Sénat, July 2001).

23. *Internet et les réseaux numériques*, Report to the Prime Minister, 1998; Christiane Feral-Schuhl, "Internet: le Conseil d'Etat prone une haute sécurité pour la consommateur," *Les Echos*, September 29, 1998.

24. "Décollage imminent de l'e-signature," *Les Echos*, April 11, 2001, p. 45.

25. Samer Iskander and David Owen, "Jospin's Decision to Free Up Use of Internet Is Welcomed," *Financial Times*, January 21, 1999, p. 6.

26. Erich Inciyan, "L'espionnage électronique, priorité de la sécurité informatique," *Le Monde*, January 21, 1999; Hervé Morin, "La France mise sur la cryptologie pour se protéger," *Le Monde*, February 23, 2000.

27. "Derrière l'écran du CSA: Les neuf sages confrontes a l'explosion numérique," *Les Echos*, January 18, 2001.

28. "French Telco Act Puts the Internet in Leash," *Lambda Bulletin*, June 13, 1996 (www.lambda.eu.org/208-html).

29. Blanca Riemer, "La loi Trautmann clarific les responsabilités sur le Web," *La Tribune*, May 27, 1999, p. 27.

30. Christian Paul, *Du droit et des libertés sur Internet*, Report to the Prime Minister (Paris: La documentation Française, 2001), p. 71.

31. Laurence Girard and Anne Marie Rocco, "Le gouvernement donne le coup d'envoi a la société de l'information," *Le Monde*, April 5, 2001.

32. Delphine Denuit, "Qui doit censurer les sites Web illégaux?" *Le Figaro*, July 12, 2001.

33. Florent Latrive, "Le 'cybermachin', pas encore né, déjà décrié," *Libération*, February 21, 2001, p. 24.

34. Michel Alberganti, "La justice reconnaît l'impossibilité de bloquer des sites d'Internet," *Le Monde*, June 14, 1996.

35. "French Telco Act Puts the Internet in Leash."

36. Cited in Shannon, "From France, Yahoo Case Resonates."

37. Florent Latrive, "Altern pourrait rouvrir en mai," *Libération*, April 23, 1999 (www.liberation.fr/multi/actu/semaine990419/art990423.html [June 18, 2001]); Guillaume Fraissard, "Des histoires qui fâchent," *Le Monde*, March 17, 1999.

38. "Les ennemis de l'Internet," *Transfert*, February 27, 2001 (www.transfert.net, June 18, 2001).

39. Joël Heslaut, "Acteurs de l'Internet, responsables mais pas coupables," *Petites Affiches* 177 (September 5, 2000), pp. 4–5; see also www.assemblee-nat.fr/2/cra/20000061521.htm.

40. Riemer, "La loi Trautmann."

41. Edgar Pansu, "La mobilisation contre l'amendement Bloche gagne du terrain," *Transfert*, June 26, 2000.

42. Yves Eudes, "La législation sur les hebergeurs de sites Internet est vivement contestée," *Le Monde*, June 8, 2000.

43. Heslaut, "Acteurs de l'Internet."

44. The legal suit was brought by Avenir de la langue Française (ALF), created in 1992, and Défense de la langue Française (DLF), created in 1958.

45. Kristi Issick, "Court Throws Out French-Language Internet Case," *IDGNet News*, April 30, 2001 (www.idg.net.nz).

46. Law no. 75-1349of December 31, 1975, *Journal Officiel*, January 4, 1976.

47. Jean-Jacques Biolay, *Le Droit de la publicité* (Paris: Presses universitaires de France, 1986), p. 66.

48. Michel Arseneault, "Les militants de la francophonie s'attaquent a Internet," *Le Monde*, December 2, 1996.

49. Constitutional law no. 92-554.

50. See www.culture.gouv.fr/culture/dglf [May 31, 2001]).

51. Annie Kahn, "La culture, à portée d'écran," *Le Monde*, February 2, 1998.

52. Interestingly, the Internet helped to highlight the multiple languages that were already being used even within France, from traditional regional languages like Breton and Provençal to the languages of relative newcomers to France, such as Romany and Arabic.

53. Stephanie Dupont, "La francophonie veut se doter d'une force de frappe politique et économique," *Les Echos*, November 13, 1997, p. 6.

54. The choice of location was not auspicious. Only 1 percent of Vietnamese speak French, owing to an aggressive government program to eradicate the country's colonial past. Vietnam even called in January 2001 for the European Union to process its documents exclusively in English. Hervé Bourges, "Comment peut-on être francophone?" *Le Monde*, November 19, 1997.

55. Yves Marie Labe, "Les pays membres de la francophonie veulent investir Internet," *Le Monde*, May 22, 1997.

56. "L'université virtuelle rapproche le Nord du Sud," *Les Echos*, October 6, 1999.

57. Kahn, "La culture, à portée d'écran."

58. Labe, "Les pays membres de la francophonie."

59. Ross Tieman, "Minitel Millions Enticed by Web," *Financial Times*, June 9, 1999, p. 12; Claude de Loupy, "Multilinguisme et document numérique: la dimension technique à l'épreuve du codage des caractères," *Solaris*, December 1999–January 2000, section 5.1 (www.info.unicaen.fr/bnum/jelec/Solaris/d06/61oupy.html [May 29, 2001]).

60. Global Reach (www.glreach.com/gbc/fr/french.php3 [May 1, 2002]).

61. Stephanie Stoll, "Next Click, France," *Guardian*, September 7, 2000, p. 7.

62. Aurora Rodríguez Aragón, Klaus W. Grewlich, and Loris Di Pietrantonio, "Competing Telecommunications and Cyber Regulation," *International Journal of Communications Law and Policy* 3 (Summer 1999), p. 6 (www.ijclp.org/3_1999/pdf/ijclp_webdoc_8_3_1999.pdf).

63. "Chirac demande un cadre juridique international"; "Hervé Bourges souhaite la création d'un 'CSA européen,'" *Les Echos*, October 17, 1995.

64. "Chirac demande un cadre juridique international."

65. Paul Meller, "Concern on Europe E-commerce," *New York Times*, February 8, 2001.

66. Paul Meller, "Europe Panel Is Rethinking How It Views E-commerce," *New York Times*, June 27, 2001.

67. "Les e-mails non sollicités bientôt hors la loi," *Les Echos*, January 7, 2001, p. 105.

68. Serge Gauthronet and Etienne Drouard, *Unsolicited Commercial Communications and Data Protection* (Brussels: Commission of the European Communities, January 2001), p. 92.

69. Ibid.

70. European Union directive 97/66/EC.

71. Alexandra Petrovic, "Le Débat sur les E-mails non sollicités reste en suspens," *La Tribune*, March 1, 2002, p. 29.

72. "Une situation juridique confuse," *La Tribune*, March 1, 2002.

73. European Union directive 2000/31/EC.

74. Gauthronet and Drouard, *Unsolicited Commercial Communications and Data Protection*, p. 92.

75. The data protection provision was Article 29 of European Union directive 95/46/EC. Unambiguous consent may include previous contact with a company; fairness of processing requires that companies have a legitimate reason for collecting the data.

76. Gauthronet and Drouard, *Unsolicited Commercial Communications and Data Protection*, p. 108.

77. Margaret Johnston, "EU Privacy Directive Would Cost U.S. Consumers," *IDG News Services*, May 1, 2001.

78. Robert E. Litan, *Balancing Costs and Benefits of New Privacy Initiatives*, Working Paper 99-3 (Washington: AEI-Brookings Joint Center for Regulatory Studies, April 1999), p. 11.

79. Ian Lynch, "Brussels Sprouts Yet More Anger over Spam," *Vnunet.com*, October 24, 2001.

80. European Union directive 2000/385 extends to e-mail the provision of directive 97/66, which prohibits commercial solicitations by fax or automated caller. This provision was transposed into French law by regulations of July 25 and August 23, 2001. Anne-Laure Béranger, "Le Conseil des ministres européens tranche en faveur d l'opt-in," *Le Journal du Net*, December 10, 2001.

81. Petrovic, "Le Débat sur les E-mails non sollicités."

82. Deborah Spar, *Ruling the Waves: Cycles of Discovery, Chaos, and Wealth from the Compass to the Internet* (Harcourt, 2001), p. 370.

83. Lawrence Lessig, *Code and Other Laws of Cyberspace* (Basic Books, 1999), p. 43.

84. "Le tribunal de Paris se déclare compétent pour juger l'ex-président de Yahoo," *Agence France-Presse*, February 26, 2002.

85. Ariane Beky, "Affaire Front14.org: Les FAI respirent!" *NetEconomie*, October 21, 2001 (www.neteconomie.com/perl/navig.pl/neteconomie/infos/article/20011031103121).

86. Ned Stafford, "French Judge Refuses to Block Racist Front 14," *Washington Post*, July 13, 2001.

Chapter Six

1. Patrick A. Messerlin, "France," in Benn Steil, David G. Victor, and Richard R. Nelson, eds., *Technological Innovation and Economic Performance* (Princeton University Press, 2002), p. 147.

2. Peter Hall and David Soskice, *Varieties of Capitalism: The Institutional Foundations of Comparative Capitalism* (Oxford University Press, 2001), pp. 38–39.

3. U.S. figures for 1999.

4. "This Risk-Taker Is Ready to Roll the Dice," *Business Week*, July 1, 2002, p. 50.

5. Adrien de Tricornot and Cécile Ducourtieux, "Les investisseurs en capital-risque réduisent la voilure," *Le Monde*, August 12, 2002.

6. Cecile Ducourtieux, "Les incubateurs publics prennent le relais du secteur prive," *Le Monde*, August 13, 2002.

7. "Les FCPI ont soutenu le capital-risque en France au premier semestre," *Les Echos*, September 17, 2002, p. 20.

8. Adrien de Tricornot, "Les capital-risqueurs ont reduit leurs investissements a 100 milliards de dollars en 2001," *Le Monde*, September 19, 2002.

9. Yasmine Chinwala, "Germany Will Not Deliver Top Returns," *eFinancialNews*, September 6, 2002.

10. European Venture Capital Association, *EVCA Yearbook 2001* (London: KPMG, 2002), p. 132.

11. Philippe Collombel, interview by the author, Paris, October 2002.

12. Pierre Kupferman, "L'Etat doit s'attaquer aux problemes d'après création," *La Tribune*, January 29, 2002, p. 29.

13. François Véron, interview by the author, Paris, October 2002.

14. Laurent Kott, interview by the author, Paris, October 2002.

15. Ifop, "Radioscopie de l'entreprise vue par les 18–40 ans," results presented at the Salon des entrepreneurs, January 31–February 2, 2002 (www.salondesentrepreneurs.com/index.asp?p=etudes01 [September 25, 2002]).

16. Stéphane Boujnah, interview by the author, Paris, October 2002.

17. Benoît Habert, Croissance Plus, interview by the author, Paris, October 2002.

18. Philippe Collombel, interview.

Index